THE
Answer
TO
Anger

JUNE HUNT

HARVEST HOUSE PUBLISHERS
EUGENE, OREGON

Cover by Garborg Design Works, Savage, Minnesota

Cover photo © pmphoto / Bigstock

Some of the names and details in this book have been changed to protect the anonymity and privacy of the individuals who shared their stories.

Formerly titled *Keeping Your Cool...When Your Anger Is Hot!*

THE ANSWER TO ANGER
Copyright © 2009, 2013 by Hope for the Heart, Inc.
Published by Harvest House Publishers
Eugene, Oregon 97402
www.harvesthousepublishers.com

ISBN 978-0-7369-4930-9 (pbk.)
ISBN 978-0-7369-4931-6 (eBook)

Library of Congress Cataloging-in-Publication Data
    Hunt, June.
    [Keeping your cool— when your anger is hot!]
    The answer to anger / June Hunt.
        pages cm
    Originally published: Keeping your cool— when your anger is hot! 2009.
    Includes bibliographical references (pages   ).
    ISBN 978-0-7369-4930-9 (pbk.)
    1. Anger—Religious aspects—Christianity. I. Title.
    BV4627.A5H87 2013
    241'.3—dc23
                                                                2012041905

Printed in the United States of America

13 14 15 16 17 18 19 20 21 / BP - JH / 10 9 8 7 6 5 4 3 2 1

Dedication

With deep respect I dedicate this book to my sister, Swanee Hunt, who has long been channeling her *indignation* over social injustice into *action*. Although we have teased about "cancelling each other's votes," we are always in each other's corner—emphatically—concerning abuse, injustice, and proactive compassion.

Swanee allowed her *justifiable anger* regarding the worldwide epidemic of sex trafficking to fuel her efforts to combat this horrendous atrocity. Her righteous indignation helped energize the movement, involving world leaders and heads of state, to rescue young women and girls who are victims of inhumane, evil sex traffickers.

Previously as ambassador from the United States to Austria, Swanee saw firsthand the aftermath of brutal savagery from the Bosnian war—the wholesale genocide of almost the entire male population in the town of Srebrenica, all fathers, sons, husbands...murdered. As a result, she assisted in the mobilization of women around the globe to take action, to become leaders, to make their world a far more civil place.

With a vision of what could be, Swanee has empowered the weak to become strong, the timid to become bold, the victim to become victorious. Indeed, she has helped the voiceless find a voice.

Swanee has refused to sit behind her mahogany desk at Harvard University and merely teach about injustices. Rather, she has rolled up her sleeves, marshaled her assets, garnered her allies, neutralized her opponents, focused her intellect, and thrown her energy into making a significant difference in the lives of those who have been disenfranchised. Swanee's anger propelled her to action...and as a result, she is changing the world.

Acknowledgments

If I were deprived of the opportunity to express in print my deepest appreciation to the dedicated team that helped make this book possible, I might be tempted to become…angry! Therefore, with heartfelt gratitude I joyfully acknowledge…

- *The firefighters of Dallas Fire Station #21, Love Field Airport:* Who provided significant insights into the essential skills of firefighting.

- *Barbara Spruill:* Whose vivid recollections of my early struggles with anger surpassed even my own memories—she lovingly sparked personal recollections of my failures and victories, which are candidly revealed throughout these pages.

- *Lillian Spruill:* Whom I affectionately refer to as "the Mother of the World," for keeping the home fires burning.

- *Keith Wall:* Whose invaluable organization of the first draft fueled our creativity.

- *Angie White, Bea Garner, Carolyn White, Elizabeth Cunningham, Jill Prohaska, Karen Williams, Phillip Bleecker, Laura Lyn Benoit, Steve Miller,* and *Titus O'Bryant* for…
  - keying and re-keying
  - editing and re-editing
  - proofing and reproofing
  - researching and re-researching

They not only performed with the utmost diligence but also fanned the flame of loving support. (You are my editorial Dream Team.)

- *Kay Yates:* Who, as my personal assistant, juggled calendars and single-handedly snuffed out brush fires—enabling the rest of our team to "keep going on all four burners."

I am genuinely blessed by God to have each of you in my life.

— *June*

Contents

PART THREE
Fighting Fire with Fire:
How to Use Anger in Healthy Ways

Introduction

God Has an Answer for Your Anger

I BECAME AWARE of the extraordinary number of people struggling with anger when I was in Arizona in the mid-1990s at Prescott
Pines Conference Center. I had been asked to be the general session
speaker for a series of four back-to-basics conferences. This was the
first time I had ever brought all of our *Biblical Counseling Keys* from
our ministry—100 practical resources that address life's toughest
problems.

For more than two weeks, I kept calling back to our office in Dallas,
Texas, asking staff to send us hundreds more of our *Biblical Counseling
Keys*. And by far the resource on anger was in greatest demand, and I
didn't even speak on that topic!

After returning from Arizona, I checked to see how our ministry
was meeting this need to help people with their anger, and I was surprised at the results. People have been requesting more of our *Biblical
Counseling Keys* on *Anger* than any other topic, just like at the conferences. Clearly, people continue to seek *real answers* for their *real
problems*. Fortunately, this book has *real solutions*!

Anger is perhaps the most mystifying and powerful emotion we
experience—and potentially the most volatile. There is much confusion about anger. We often become conflicted over the *should nots* and
oughts...like "good people *should not* have any anger" and "you *ought*
to get rid of all anger—immediately."

Typically we don't want to acknowledge any anger within us, so...

we stuff it, disguise it, medicate it, rename it, anesthetize it—but that only adds fuel to the fire burning deep within.

In truth, anger is like a red light on the dashboard of your car—a warning light that indicates something is wrong and needs your attention. God's design for anger is to caution us, not to control us...and to ultimately cause us to think about options that will bring about positive change.

᛭

As uncomfortable as it is, I don't know of any other way to write this book on anger—with total integrity—without being candid about my own struggle with it...especially in my younger years. This means I need to speak about personal events and painful people from my past. Therefore, when I do so, it isn't to be dramatic, but rather to be authentic. My intent is not to hurt, but rather to help. That is my sincere prayer.

Learning about anger has been a journey I've been on most of my adult life...and oh, what I've learned! I've walked through the burning embers of my own suppressed anger, and I've also learned how to take shelter from the explosive, fiery anger of others. Now I want to help you discover the same invaluable lessons I've learned.

From personal experience, I have every confidence that, with God's help, you can find the answer to anger and enjoy a peaceful life.

Part One

Fanning the Embers:

The Truth About Anger and
How It Affects Our Lives

The Anger Bowl

The Overwhelming Pain of Our Anger

"Get rid of all bitterness, rage and anger"
(Ephesians 4:31).

It's too much. The pain is just too much!" cried a voice seething with anger. "I'm so upset...so angry...my life has turned into a living hell."

- *The place*: the mountains of Prescott, Arizona
- *The occasion*: a weekend retreat for more than 600 women
- *The setting*: an outdoor pavilion with a large stone fireplace

On a Friday evening, after I had just finished speaking, a distraught woman came forward, baring her soul. Actually, Brenda was supported—practically *carried*—by three deeply concerned friends. As she reached out, I took her hands and led her to sit down by me. She was overwrought with emotion.

Initially, Brenda didn't want to talk with me. In fact, she didn't want to attend the conference at all. But her friends knew how desperately she needed some kind of intervention—something to pull her out of this emotional "pit," something to get her back on level ground.

"Brenda, please tell me what happened. I can see you're in pain."

Immediately she blurted out, "My daughter died of anorexia*... she was just 22!" Heaving sobs poured out between every phrase. "She meant the world to me...she had so much potential...so much future...she was vibrant...and so precious...then she withered...withered away—to nothing."

At the word *nothing*, Brenda's body wilted and she began to wail. I now understood the source of this mother's agony. It was the tragedy of watching her daughter die of self-imposed starvation—shrinking to skin and bones, unaware of her own distorted thoughts...thinking she was much too fat when instead she was much too thin...thinking she was eating too much when instead she was slowly starving.

Within moments, the picture was plain to me. Brenda was emotionally confined in a fiery pit—a pit of anger. It was as though this pit contained hot coals that she could pick up and hurl at any time, pelting those who angered her. Yet she hadn't realized she was the one being burned.

Brenda was consumed with agonizing anger, a bitter wrath...

- *at her husband*—for not taking the problem seriously
  —"She's just going through a phase."
- *at her friends*—for not showing compassion, but stating trite comments
  —"She's cute and trim and doesn't want to be fat!"
- *at her family*—for not understanding the real issues
  —"Just make her eat!"
- *at her doctors*—for not being more proactive
  —"Don't worry. I'm watching her."

---

*Anorexia is a psychological eating disorder characterized by compulsive, chronic self-starvation.[1] It is a disorder in which the normal function of the mind and/or body is disturbed. Anorexics weigh less than their ideal body weight, which is different for every person (based on bone structure and the amount of muscle). Body weight that is 15 percent below normal poses a serious threat to a person's physical health.[2]

- *at her hospital*—for not supplying lifesaving solutions
  —"We're doing all we can."
- *at herself*—for not knowing what to do sooner
  —"Why didn't I spend even more time searching for solutions?"
- *at her God*—for not rescuing her precious child
  —"Why didn't God stop this senseless tragedy?"
- *at her daughter*—for not fighting to live, not trying to change, for withering away to nothing, for leaving her, for dying
  —"I can't believe how her destructive choices have forever devastated me."

"I am so very sorry, Brenda. When did your daughter die?" Her answer surprised me. "It's been over three years now...but it still feels like yesterday."

Rarely have I met someone so ravaged by sorrow. My heart hurt for her as I silently cried out to God on her behalf.

For over half an hour, Brenda and I sat together on the first row of that pavilion. Continuing to ask questions, I heard more of her anguishing story—her years of reaching out to her daughter, her countless hours of prayer, her sleepless nights of worry, her failed attempts to find help.

When she finished pouring out her heart, I said, "Brenda, you can find true healing. Though your world feels so painful right now, you can receive real relief from that pain. You may not see it, but there is hope for your heart."

She looked at me as if she wanted to believe, but she had been disappointed so many times it was difficult for her to trust my words.

At that very moment, the Lord put into my mind a symbolic picture of what Brenda could do with her pain. I asked her to cup her hands together in the shape of a bowl. Then I asked her to imagine writing on slips of paper each specific hurt, the names of each person who had caused pain, and each angering moment. I then instructed her to imagine placing these slips of paper one by one into her "anger bowl."

Brenda seemed more than eager to get it all out. Together we verbally "wrote down" every feeling of helplessness, hurt, and heartache related to the death of her daughter. Her sorrow, pain, and anger were so extensive, she agonized to recall each incident as we gathered them into her imaginary bowl.

I believed that Brenda had likely been carrying the burden of anger long before her daughter's eating disorder. My aim was for her to leave the Arizona mountains *totally* free of the charred memories from childhood on up. I asked Brenda to again imagine writing down the names of the people and events throughout her life that caused her anger and pain not related to her daughter's illness and death, and to place those slips of paper in her anger bowl as well.

"Ask God to bring every person and event to mind so you can find complete healing," I gently prodded. "Include even the 'little' hurts that could still be lingering."

When the last "slip of paper" dropped into the bowl, I asked Brenda if she wanted to keep carrying all that anger or if she wanted to release it. "Oh, I want to release it all. I've carried this anger far too long as it is."

Giving a Sacrificial Offering to God

"Now I want you to take this anger bowl over to the fireplace," I explained, "and empty it all into the fire."

"I really want to empty the bowl," she quickly responded. "I *really need* to empty the bowl."

Putting my hands under her hands, I softly said, "Let me help you." Carefully we both carried the figuratively heavy bowl. "Brenda, although you felt you had the right to be angry, you can now present all your anger to the Lord as a *sacrificial* offering." She nodded. Staring at the fire, she paused, then prayed, "I release my anger bowl to You."

Slowly separating her hands...then slowly turning them over...she "poured" the contents of the bowl into the fire and allowed her anger to be consumed by the flames. Then, with the palms of her hands still over the fire, she spontaneously began moving her fingers up and down—making sure no "slips of paper" clung to her, making sure no sliver of anger remained.

As Brenda presented her burnt offering to the Lord, I believe the God of heaven and Earth received it as a sacrifice to Him. He blew away her anger like light ash on a cool breeze. He truly lightened her load.

After the conference had drawn to a close on that Sunday afternoon, Brenda's friends rushed up to me, full of excitement. "Have you seen Brenda today?"

"No, I haven't seen her since Friday night." Then they began gushing, their words overlapping one another: "It's amazing...she's joyful... she's glowing...she's radiant!"

Then one exclaimed, "Stay here! We'll bring her to you."

Off they scurried...and within five minutes, the flock of four returned. No doubt about it—their exuberant words were right. Brenda's face was beaming—her eyes bright, her countenance beautiful.

The reason? Brenda's anger bowl was completely empty. She had emptied her heart of all past hurt, all past pain, all past anger. She had yielded her right to hold on to her list of resentments, and had presented her offering to the Lord. She knew He was well pleased.

It was amazing to see how an anger that had smoldered for years could be snuffed out in such a relatively short time. Brenda's consuming coals of anger had been cooled by the breath of God.

※

Do You Need to Bring a Burnt Offering?

Has anger seethed in your soul for so long that you sincerely question, "Can it really be contained? Can it be completely extinguished? Can this powerful emotion truly be transformed from adversary to ally?"

The answer is unequivocally *yes*. But, as with Brenda, your starting point will probably be filling your own "anger bowl," then allowing God's purifying fire to burn away the blistering pain that for too long has been harming you and those you love.

If you are tempted to think, *But I have every right to be angry! It's too high a price to let go*, reflect on these words in the Bible: "I will not sacrifice to the LORD my God burnt offerings that cost me nothing."[3]

Realize that Jesus promises to be your burden bearer. He gives hope to the hopeless and help to the helpless. Instead of casting hot coals on the people who have angered you, do as the Bible says: "Cast all your anxiety on him because he cares for you." [4]

Every time you pick up burning coals to pelt people who have hurt you, know this: It's like lighting yourself on fire and waiting for the other person to burn.

2

Turning Up the Heat

The Four Intensities of Our Anger

*"Do not be quickly provoked in your spirit,
for anger resides in the lap of fools"*
(ECCLESIASTES 7:9).

I HAVE A confession: For a number of years, I struggled with an anger problem. I had an anger bowl filled with many slips of paper, but there was only one name written on all of them—*Dad*.

In terms of expressing anger, it's probably not what you think. I've never been a dish thrower, a wall puncher, or a fist shaker. Far from it. And my voice, even when I'm angry, doesn't reach high decibels.

My problem with anger stemmed from total ignorance: first, in having no understanding about it; and second, in not knowing how to handle it. I considered anger as being something that was always bad—an emotion to be *avoided* when it flared in others, an emotion to be *extinguished* when it flared in me.

Recently, when I discussed these thoughts with a close friend, she reminded me of how I typically dealt with anger—even as a young adult.

"You used to hide behind doors," she recalled.

"Whenever you would hear your dad walking toward the room you were in, you'd slide behind the door rather than run the risk of facing his rage. Even if he wasn't in a bad mood, you made sure you avoided him to stay out of harm's way."

My friend's comment basically captured how I responded to anger, or even the possibility of it. I'd try to get out of the way—walk, run, hide, whatever! But what I didn't realize was that resentful slips of paper were accumulating in my anger bowl.

My "disappearing act" concerning my dad goes back to childhood. I was raised in a family that clearly had—to use the vernacular— "anger issues." My father was admired by many, primarily for being a brilliant businessman and a super patriot because he was an avid anticommunist. However, he was as *deficient* in his personal skills as he was *efficient* in his professional skills. Sadly, his private life brought pain to most people around him.

When it came to anger, my father was a powder keg always on the verge of explosion. And worse, no one ever knew what might be the match that would light the fuse. For example, one Saturday afternoon, my sister Helen and I were sitting on the floor playing chess in a tiny room off of our living room. I remember hearing my father's heavy footsteps coming closer…and closer. We became ever so quiet.

When the footsteps stopped, there he stood, towering over the two of us. We looked up at him…and waited…and waited. He kept staring at the chess set.

Finally, he spewed, "PUT THAT CHESS SET UP! DON'T YOU KNOW CHECKERS IS MUCH MORE SCIENTIFIC THAN CHESS!"

Immediately my blood began to boil. Talk about "turning up the heat"! I screamed back (in total silence), "Checkers is NOT more scientific than chess!" Helen and I dared not speak a word.

In slow, slow motion, we removed each chess piece from the board. The king had bellowed his orders. We two pawns complied. We knew not to counter him, and yet another slip of paper was deposited into my anger bowl.

The following Scripture verse aptly depicts the unhealthy family dynamic that ruled our household and smothered our joy: "A king's wrath is like the roar of a lion; he who angers him forfeits his life."[1] To this day, I remember my father's *exact* words from the sabotaged chess match—both his (roaring) and mine (silence).

I've often described my upbringing as "walking on eggshells." Yet, more accurately, it was like walking through a minefield. I felt I had to tiptoe around, placing one foot cautiously in front of the other so as not to trigger an explosion.

One specific event had the greatest impact in forming my fearful attitude toward anger, and it occurred when I stepped out from behind the proverbial "door." My dad had been romantically involved with numerous women, and it wasn't exactly a secret. There came a time when I felt he needed to be confronted!

I stood before my father, determined and fully motivated by my righteous indignation (although I didn't know that term at the time). My approach was accusatory, noting his trampling on moral ground…"How could you…?" I challenged. He dismissed my words with, "I'm *not* a Christian. I *don't* have to go by Christian ethics!" Then came an outrageous allegation that Mother was mentally ill. I followed with a sarcastic remark, and he countered by inflicting multiple blows to my back—end of "discussion"!

The result of my confrontation? The next day I was promptly sent to boarding school, where I was forced to live for several months. I was exiled from family…expelled from home…punished for *confronting my dad with the truth*. Although the school was only ten minutes from our house, I was prohibited from setting foot inside our home. That crushed my mother. She felt responsible for what happened, yet was powerless to change it.

The only time I had attempted to use anger for a "worthy cause" went woefully wrong. It was an experience that left an indelible impression, to say the least, and translated into one of the deepest wounds in my heart.

And because of my "boarding school banishment," I developed my own personal style of anger management—I became a "peace at any price" person. I did whatever I could to keep the peace to avoid any eruption of anger from others.

In retrospect, by suppressing my true emotions and stifling my sincere convictions, I squelched the person God created me to be. And I unwittingly contributed to an extremely unhealthy family dynamic.

> While anger has a legitimate purpose in certain situations, it must always be handled with great caution and care.

What can we do when we find ourselves facing angry people and angry feelings of our own that we feel we can't express? To arrive at an answer, we must first learn some basics about anger.

Anger 101

What Is Anger?

Anger is a strong emotion of irritation, agitation, or hostility that occurs when a need or expectation is not met.[2] Actually, anger is a *secondary response* to something else—it's an upsetting emotional reaction to an assumed "right" that has been violated or not fulfilled.

Of all our emotions, anger is often considered the strongest, rawest, and potentially most destructive. We all know people who would fit this description: "An angry [person] stirs up dissension, and a hot-tempered one commits many sins" (Proverbs 29:22).

Now let's focus on the word *expectation*. When we expect something, we feel we have the *right* for that something to happen. And when it doesn't, we can feel irritated...agitated...ANGRY. Who hasn't been there, done that? I know I have. Unmet expectations can be the igniter when it comes to anger.

In the Old Testament, the most frequently used Hebrew word for anger is *aph*, literally meaning "nose" or "nostrils"—figuratively depicting nostrils flaring in anger. Later, *aph* came to represent the entire face as seen in two ancient Hebrew idioms:[3]

- *"Long of face"* (or nose) means "slow to anger." Psalm 145:8 describes God as slow to anger—He is not quickly provoked: "The LORD is gracious and compassionate, slow to anger and rich in love."
- *"Short of face"* (or nose) means "quick to anger." Proverbs 14:17 describes a man with anger that pops off like a firecracker: "A quick-tempered man does foolish things."

While anger has a legitimate purpose in certain situations, it must always be handled with great caution and care. As the writer of Proverbs said, "Do not make friends with a hot-tempered man, do not associate with one easily angered."[4] Why? Because someone could, and usually does, get burned by fiery rage. God might as well have said, "Thou shalt not play with fire."

What Are the Different Types of Anger?

Many people assume only one type of anger exists: Hot!

But the word *anger* actually covers four levels of emotional heat, much like a ventilator hood over a stove covers four burners. Imagine that these burners are indignation, wrath, fury, and rage.

Burner #1—*Indignation is "simmering anger"* provoked by something that appears unjust or unkind and thus the emotion seems *justified*. At times the unrighteous religious rulers in the Bible felt indignation over

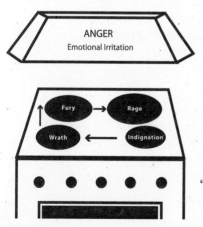

Jesus' miracles and His claim to be the Messiah; therefore, they felt justified in wanting to kill Him.[5] Their perceptions, of course, were unjustified.

Meanwhile, Jesus felt *righteous indignation* toward the religious rulers for their hardened hearts. Likewise, Jesus became "indignant" when the disciples prevented people from bringing their children to Him so He might touch and bless them: "When Jesus saw this, he was indignant. He said to them, 'Let the little children come to me, and do not hinder them, for the kingdom of God belongs to such as these.'"[6]

Burner #2—*Wrath is "burning anger"* accompanied by a desire to avenge. Wrath often moves from the inner feeling of anger to the outer expression of anger. Vengeful anger can be deadly—both literally and figuratively. An old Chinese proverb says, "The man who opts for revenge should dig two graves."

In the Bible, God expresses His wrath as divine judgment on those who commit willful sin: "The wrath of God is being revealed from heaven against all the godlessness and wickedness of men who suppress the truth by their wickedness."[7]

Burner #3—*Fury is "fiery anger"* so fierce that it destroys common sense. The word *fury* suggests a powerful force compelled to harm or destroy. Respected theologian A.W. Tozer said, "The fury of man never furthered the glory of God."[8]

Some of the religious rulers were so angry with Peter and the other apostles for proclaiming that Jesus was God, "they were furious and wanted to put them to death."[9] This is an example of why the Bible says, "Anger is cruel and fury overwhelming."[10]

Burner #4—*Rage is "blazing anger"* that results in loss of self-control, often to the extreme of heinous violence and temporary insanity. After an outburst of rage, a cry of remorseful regret or disbelief is often expressed: "I can't believe I did that!"

Yet those who continue to vent their rage toward others, including toward God, find themselves defeated by their own destructive decisions and ruined relationships. "A man's own folly ruins his life, yet his heart rages against the LORD."[11]

Anger's Progression of Intensity

Anger, if not resolved, can move from one stage of intensity to another—from mild irritation to uncontrollable rage.

- Unresolved irritation leads to indignation—*justifiably* feeling and/or acting so that a wrong is made right.
- Unresolved indignation leads to wrath—*reacting* with revenge.
- Unresolved wrath leads to fury—*reacting* with a furious lack of self-control.
- Unresolved fury leads to rage—*reacting* with unrestrained violence and a temporary loss of sanity.

The School of Life

There is no way you can graduate from the school of life without recognizing the positives and the negatives of anger.

Forest rangers are trained to fight forest fires, and they know how to "start a fire to stop a fire." Known as *backfires*, these deliberately set fires help deprive wildfires of fuel so firefighters can better contain the blaze.

God works with your anger in much the same way. He may use a recent incident of anger to spark *an awareness of the larger blaze* (your unresolved past anger) that may be impeding your emotions and hindering your relationships.

How Can Anger Be "Good"?

Anger is a surprisingly improbable instructor, teaching us what we need to be aware of, think about, and reconsider.

The Bible says, "All things work together for good to those who love God, to those who are the called according to His purpose."[12] This means not just all *positive* things, all *right* things, all *wonderful* things work together for our good...but literally *all* things. When we release all of the hurt, injustice, fear, and frustration in our lives to the Lord,

He promises to use it *all* in some way for good—even if we don't see how that is possible.

Consider your life from God's perspective. Anger can teach you to...

Address the Past
- enabling you to recognize your buried anger
- providing insight into past hurts
- motivating you to seek healing for past hurts

Address the Present
- bringing your true feelings to light
- revealing inappropriate efforts to get your needs met
- alerting you to current problems that should be addressed

Address Your Relationships
- enabling you to protect yourself and others from injustice
- exposing your need to set healthy boundaries
- inviting closeness within your relationships

Address Your Spiritual Life
- helping you realize your need for a relationship with God
- leading you to apply biblical principles for overcoming anger
- encouraging you to display a Christlike response by handling your anger properly

Over the years I've had a change of heart—a paradigm shift—in my perspective about anger. I've come to realize anger is a God-given emotion and can be a perfectly normal response mechanism. Yet anger is also an ally that can become an adversary if we don't handle it carefully. There is a mean and ugly side to it—a side that tears down rather than builds up. Unfortunately, "mean and ugly" is no doubt the most pervasive kind of anger in our world.

While it's true there are scriptures that tell us anger can be a positive influence, there are even more that warn against a negative, harmful mishandling of it. King Sol-

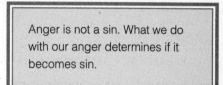

Anger is not a sin. What we do with our anger determines if it becomes sin.

omon said, "Do not be quickly provoked in your spirit, for anger resides in the lap of fools."[13]

You may have heard the saying, "The word *anger* is one letter short of *danger*." It's true—our hot-blooded emotions can land us in dangerous territory. No one who has had an encounter with out-of-control anger would deny that.

Do You Need an Anger Awakening?

Now that you've heard a bit about my journey down Anger Avenue, let me ask you: Where are you on this journey? Is anger a problem in your life? Or have you been on the receiving end of someone's anger... perhaps once too often? Are you trying to intervene before things get any worse? Is your own anger damaging relationships and causing you regrets? Chances are that you, like Brenda, have an anger bowl in your life that needs to be emptied.

The most surprising aspect of my "anger awakening" was a straightforward command found in Ephesians 4:26 (NKJV): "Be angry, and do not sin." Since I did not grow up reading the Bible, I can assure you, the concept "be angry" was both perplexing and mystifying.

How could this principle be correct when so many verses in the Bible tell us to, in essence, "turn away anger"?[14] The answer lies in understanding *what kind of anger* we carry in our hearts. For example, Jesus had justifiable anger or righteous indignation, which motivated Him to *right a wrong* when He drove the money changers from the temple because of their fraudulent practices.

Another shocker—for someone who thought anger was always wrong—is the irrefutable truth that anger is a God-given emotion. The Bible never says anger, in and of itself, is bad. Anger is not a sin. What we *do* with our anger determines if it becomes sin.

Now think about this: If God considered anger a sin, then He would have been a flagrant sinner Himself because there are more than 200 references to God's anger and wrath in the Old Testament alone. Because Scripture calls us to be godly, we can follow God's example and express justifiable anger—the kind that seeks to right a wrong.

Surely it is okay—even honorable—to feel anger in unjust situations. It's *how we handle* our natural feelings of anger that can be constructive or destructive. Anger is like many things in life that can be used for either good or bad. A knife can be used for good or for bad. It can be used for healing in the hands of a surgeon or for harm in the hands of a murderer.

In short, the *existence* of anger isn't wrong. But the *expression* of it can be.

⁂

That is why we need to discover positive, proactive ways to keep anger from raging out of control—a plan to keep our anger from becoming a danger...to ourselves and to others.

3

Fuel for the Fire
The Four Sources of Our Anger

"Fools vent their anger, but the wise quietly hold it back"
(PROVERBS 29:11 NLT).

HOW MY HEART hurt for Philip as we spoke during *Hope In The Night*, our live two-hour call-in counseling program. He was in desperate need of help.

In a tense tone, Philip described how his father, a godly minister, had been murdered by his own cousin, Jack, 19 years earlier when Philip was a teenager. Philip's dad had taken in Jack's children, who had been sexually abused by their father. One day, after a church social, Philip's father returned home and was confronted by Jack, who was angry because he hadn't been included in the family festivities. A violent argument ensued. When it was over, Philip's father lay dead, shot to death just inside his own back door and surrounded by horrified, helpless family members.

Jack spent ten years in prison for his crime, and then spent the remaining five years of his life taunting and terrorizing Philip's family with ongoing threats of deadly retribution. When Jack died, Philip wondered if the gnawing anger that had come to define his life would be laid to rest too. It was not. In fact, it steadily worsened.

Jack, it turns out, was buried just yards from Philip's "best friend"—his beloved father. Every trip to the cemetery rekindled the embers embedded in Philip's angry heart. Frustrated and exhausted, Philip told me he was desperate for change, but didn't know where to start. He wasn't even sure if help and healing were possible, given the severity of his wound. Could Philip's clenched fists unfold to form a bowl, and could the bowl possibly be large enough to contain all of his angry memories so that one day he could release them?

Here's a portion of our on-air conversation:

Philip: "I've never been able to get over my dad's death…I can't get the anger out. Jack shattered our family. Now that I'm getting older, it's getting worse. I'm so angry inside."

June: "Are you saying you tend to overreact to things that should be fairly minor?"

Philip: "Oh, all the time."

June: "Philip, this is powerful pain you're describing. I especially appreciate your call because, often, what we focus on is *what we become*. Have you considered that the very thing that caused the death of your father—his cousin's anger—is what you're struggling with now? Do you want to be like your cousin?"

Philip: "No!"

June: "Of course not. But when we aim our resentment toward another person, our heart is not focused on what is good…we're just focusing on the bad. Scripture says, 'As [a man] thinketh…so is he.'[1] So we become bitter and unforgiving. We don't know what to do with our emotions because we haven't figured out a healthy way of handling the pain."

Philip: "I just don't feel like justice was served."

June: "In truth, many people want revenge after an injustice. They want to get even. So let me ask you: Is there anything you could do now that would make it 'even'?"

Philip: "Probably not."

June: "No. You're talking about the man you loved more than all others, the one who invested his life in you. There's nothing that could *ever* make that even."

The Four Sources That Fuel Anger's Fire

Clearly, at this point in time, Philip was being ravaged by his own smoldering anger. To quench the flame, he would need to examine the sources of his anger and deal courageously with each one.

Suppose that a chair in your home catches fire. You wouldn't apply water to the smoke or to the tops of the flames. No, you'd grab an extinguisher and aim squarely at the burning cushions—toward the source of the blaze.

That's the approach we must take to quench the fire of our anger. Anger, you see, is a *secondary* emotion. It always comes from *somewhere*, but too often we can't see past the smoke and flames—a rude driver, a gossiping "friend," a procrastinating spouse, or tragically, in Philip's case, a horrible injustice—to identify the true source.

Unless we address our anger at its source: *injustice, fear, hurt,* or *frustration*, it will continue to burn us—and others. Unless we are able to release all the anger in our bowl, we'll never find lasting peace. So let's examine each of the four sources of anger, one by one.

Source #1—How Can Injustice Ignite Anger?

Growing up, I despised my father and adored my mother. She was everything he wasn't. When he tore into people with harsh, hateful words, she waited for the opportunity to say soothing words of healing.

To me, my father was the epitome of cruelty, and my mother was the epitome of kindness. I had a mountainous pile of angry memories of my father, and nary a one of my mother.

So when he treated her unjustly, I would become indignant at the unfairness of it all and determined to make him see how wrong he was. After all, someone had to set him straight and come to my mother's defense!

Of course, my lofty aspirations far exceeded my ability to bring about real change. And my feeble efforts to confront my father's infidelity only landed me in boarding school, which only increased my mother's suffering. The lesson learned: Never confront my father again about his unjust treatment of anyone, not even my mother. Instead, I harbored hateful thoughts toward him for years.

The novelist Charles Dickens wrote in *Great Expectations*, "In the little world in which children have their existence, whosoever brings them up, there is nothing so finely perceived and so finely felt as injustice."[2]

How true! Even children who don't know the word *rights* are very articulate when it comes to arguing for their right to a toy or their fair share of ice cream. We are born with a well-defined sense of the things and treatment we think we are entitled to—an awareness we never lose in life.

We who are part of Western society are among the most rights-oriented people in history. We have bravely championed civil rights, human rights, women's rights, animal rights, voting rights, and property rights. This includes the right to free speech, free assembly, and free religious expression—and rightly so! What, then, do we feel when our rights, or those of someone we care about, have been violated? We feel *angry*—and that's not necessarily a bad thing.

As with anything that fuels our anger, however, there is danger in letting our outrage grow to such proportions that it erupts like a volcano with a flow of regrettable consequences. There is an immense difference between mounting a campaign to legislate against injustice and picking up a gun to shoot those who perpetuate injustice.

God asks us to surrender our "right" to handle injustice in our own way to the Savior, who *is* "the Way." He alone knows how to right every wrong. And, someday, He will.

Source #2—How Can Fear Ignite Anger?

Money, they say, is power. In my younger years, that belief kept me in constant fear of my financially successful father. Whenever his multiple marital affairs and harsh treatment left my mother in tears, he asserted, "Tears are a sign of mental illness." On numerous occasions he took her to be evaluated by a psychiatrist.

Knowing mentally ill people were often hospitalized for long periods of time, I lived in constant fear of coming home from school one day and finding that my mother had been taken away to be hospitalized by some doctor my father had paid off.

As a result, I made sure I never cried. And I began a "defense fund" for my mother in case my father ever had her declared mentally ill. I wanted to be ready to hire a lawyer to get her out of the hospital. I put in this fund every penny, nickel, dime, and quarter I could come up with—including regularly stealing a few coins from the loose change my father left on his night table.

> Fear is potent fuel for runaway anger, but a commitment to cling to God's fear-quenching love is more potent by far.

The fear of my father was in equilibrium with my anger toward him. And even though I never needed to use my "defense fund," it was years before I would let myself cry or spend the money I had meticulously saved.

Fear is potent fuel for runaway anger, but a commitment to cling to God's fear-quenching love is more potent by far. The Bible explains it this way: "There is no fear in love. But perfect love drives out fear."[3] Yet it would be years before I encountered this kind of divine love. In the meantime, my anger smoldered.

Source #3—How Can Hurt Ignite Anger?

Think back to the last time you hit your thumb with a hammer or whacked your head on a low-hanging kitchen cabinet. I can guarantee your reaction was immediate—the intense pain you felt was quickly followed by a surge of anger.

Anger follows pain for one reason: to help you make the cause of the hurt go away. It's a useful and necessary response. If you accidentally hit yourself with the hammer, your momentary anger is directed *inward*. "I can't believe I did that! Be more careful! Watch what you're doing!" If someone else is attacking you with a hammer, your anger is focused *outward* in fear—preparing you to eliminate the threat by either fighting back or running away. That's called the fight-or-flight response.

The exact same anger reflex occurs when we are hurt *emotionally*. The difference is that sometimes the cause (hurt) and effect (anger) are not so clearly linked. Physical pain is straightforward: "I'm angry—you just slapped my face! Don't you dare do it again!" But emotional wounds are more subtle, and we deal with them differently—less directly. Typically we try to ignore them, blame ourselves for them, or privately nurse them...for long periods of time.

Physical pain rarely makes us feel like a failure or a fool, but we're frequently embarrassed or ashamed of our emotional hurts. As a result, we are prone to leave our heartaches unattended, and then they start piling up like deadwood in a dry forest. There they become fuel for the kind of anger that is no longer beneficial, but dangerous and needlessly destructive. It sets the stage for explosive behavior that we didn't even know was in us.

In my own life, my three siblings and I had virtually no personal relationship with our father. We never climbed up in his lap or reached out for his hand. We never heard "I love you," or "I believe in you." We were never tucked into bed or given a good-night kiss by him. We never shared our hopes and dreams with him or sought his counsel or comfort when troubled.

We occupied the same house, but did not share a home.

Were it not for our mother, we would have been void of any emotional nurturing, spiritual encouragement, or physical affection. We had a father but never a daddy, a provider but never a protector, a critic but never a confidant, a bully but never a hero. The void I experienced was deadening, the hurt was demeaning, and the anger was damaging. Over time my anger bowl deepened and widened to accommodate one painful incident after another.

Source #4—How Can Frustration Ignite Anger?

Compared to the powerful emotional impact of injustice, fear, and hurt, the fourth cause of anger—frustration—seems to be less substantive. But consider this: Each of us has a vision of the way life "should be." In other words, we have *expectations* of happiness, comfort, success, and security. Even in mundane matters we want blue skies and smooth sailing. Checkbooks should always balance, drains should never back up, and cars should never break down.

Of course, we all know life's not like that. Troubles seem to find us no matter how hard we try to avoid them. Frustration that becomes problematic arises when our expectations are consistently unmet over time. Then it's easy to find ourselves simmering on a slow burn.

After a while we stop *getting* angry at particular frustrations and we start *being* angry as a lifestyle. And within every angry person is a bundle of kindling needing only a small match to ignite a blaze far hotter than the frustration ever warrants. Frustrated expectations and desires are volatile fuel for unrestrained anger.

I learned early in life that no child is a match for an adult, and I was certainly no match for my father. Yet I hoped against hope that someone would be able and willing to rise to the occasion and "take him down" a notch or two and rescue us from his tyrannical rule. But no knight from King Arthur's Round Table, no Superman, no defender of the people ever showed up to free us.

I knew my father was wrong. But I also knew I was powerless to change him or the circumstances. Nevertheless, I knew right should prevail over wrong and good over evil, but that wasn't happening in my home, in my family, or with my father.

Something had to be done, but nothing was being done. Nothing I could conceive or contrive would help—nothing, that is, short of murder, the ultimate anger slip in my overflowing anger bowl.

As bizarre as it may sound to most people—but probably not all—I was only trying to stop the pain. This was the only way I thought a "final solution" might be possible. One day I approached my mother with the concept—"Mom, I have figured out a way to kill Dad." In my teenage mind, I was simply being loyal and using my human logic. However, she calmly assured me, "No, honey, I appreciate what you're trying to do, but that really won't be necessary."

Where did my morbid "solution" come from? It was borne out of my unmet expectations and frustration. I was a captive of my own making, a prisoner of my own unmet desires. But not until I was an adult would I realize that sobering fact.

We can keep from fanning the flames of frustration by surrendering all our unmet expectations to the perfect will of God, thereby recognizing He is in control of every circumstance and has a perfect plan for our lives. But until we let God's will reign over our own will—based on our own expectations—our frustration-based anger will continue to burn.

In my own personal story, it's easy to find all four causes of anger at work. Hurt, injustice, fear, and frustration were all emblazoned in my spirit and it would take a while to extinguish them from my life.

In Search of Healing

Emotional Debridement

As we revisit Philip's story, it seems that friends, family, and a lifetime of Bible training told him he needed to let go of his anger and forgive. But thus far, he'd been completely powerless to do so. The tragic death of his father had produced an ugly, oozing wound. Left unattended, it had festered for years—devastating his soul...draining his spirit. Total healing called for spiritual surgery.

When dealing with a burn wound, those charged with treating

it have to carry out a painful and unwelcome process called *debride-ment*, during which outer layers of crusty deposits are removed. This allows air to reach the innermost part of the wound—ensuring lasting healing from the inside out. Debridement is anything but pleasant. It requires revisiting, exposing, and cleansing the wound. But if it's not done correctly, a burn wound will never completely heal.

With this in mind, I began to gently lead Philip through a process of spiritual and emotional debridement, prayerfully asking the Great Physician to bring healing.

June: "Philip, anger is actually a secondary response to one of four underlying injuries: hurt, injustice, fear, or frustration. I'd like for us to look at each one, beginning with hurt. How would you characterize the hurt that surrounded your father's death?"

Philip: "It was the absolute most you could ever hurt anybody. It was that bad."

June: "That's completely understandable. Now let's consider the second cause of anger—injustice."

Philip: "A ten-year sentence wasn't enough for premeditated murder. I can't reconcile it."

June: "Absolutely not. That is one hundred percent unjust. Your dad did not do anything to provoke this. What about fear? Did your ordeal bring any sense of fear of the future?"

Philip: "Jack sent letters from prison saying he was gonna kill all of us when he got out. He lived nearly five years after his release. During that time, my mother and I moved out of state because we were so afraid."

June: "Okay, so you're telling me you experienced hurt, injustice, and fear. What about frustration? Did you feel frustrated over the situation?"

Philip: "I still do, every single day."

June: "Philip, I feel for you so deeply. And I have a better understanding now about why anger has taken root in your life. But holding on to this anger will only be detrimental to you."

Phillip: "June, I can't see where he deserves forgiveness."

June: "Unforgiveness is going to keep you in prison just as surely as Jack was in prison. Forgiveness sets the prisoner free. I'm glad you used the word *deserve* because forgiveness is not based on what is deserved. Forgiveness means that you are giving what is not deserved. The Bible, in Colossians 3:13, says, 'Bear with each other and forgive whatever grievances you have against one another. Forgive as the Lord forgave you.'

> Forgiveness is not letting the guilty off the hook; it is moving the guilty from your hook to God's hook.

"Forgiveness is not circumventing God's justice; it is allowing God to execute His justice in His time and in His way. Forgiveness is not letting the guilty off the hook; it is moving the guilty from your hook to God's hook. Forgiveness is not excusing unjust behavior; it's acknowledging that unjust behavior is without excuse, while still forgiving. Forgiveness is not based on what is fair; it wasn't fair for Jesus to hang on the cross, but He did so that we could be forgiven. Is this making sense so far…?"

Philip: "It is. It really is."

June: "Think of it this way: Forgiveness is not a feeling; it is a choice. It's an act of the will. And the problem is this: If you do not forgive, the choice you have made is to become bitter and angry and then you become like the one who did the most damage to your life. You're finding you now have anger that is out of control. That's exactly what Jack had—anger out of control. Is that correct?"

Philip: "That is true."

June: "When Jesus hung on the cross, He said, 'Father, forgive them'— meaning He had a heart of forgiveness. Do you want to be like Jesus? Do you want to be Christlike? Is that important to you?"

Philip: "Oh yes, that's everything I want to be."

June: "That means you're going to need to find a way to forgive, and there's going to be a huge emotional release when you do. Forgiveness not only means dismissing the debt, it means dismissing negative emotions toward others, such as resentment. This has been tough for you, and I understand why. But it's ultimately releasing your right to hear, 'I'm sorry.' You release your right to be bitter, to get even, to dwell on the offense. You release your resentment toward the offender and the penalty you think he deserves."

Dousing the Flames Through Forgiveness

Philip and I talked for two hours that night, live, on the radio. During our remaining time together, I explained more about the biblical basis for forgiveness (which I cover at length in my book *How to Forgive...When You Don't Feel Like It*). I asked Philip to list as many specific hurts as he could that were related to his father's death.

Philip recounted each painful offense—representing his burdens and bitterness—the loss of his beloved father, his mother's resulting health problems, his inability to trust, his anxiety about the future, the strained relationship with his wife...one by one he listed them. There had been more than enough "fuel for the fire" for Philip to hold on to a lifetime of bitterness—even hatred.

Once he'd recounted every last grievance and hurt, I asked Philip two crucial questions: "Do you want to keep Jack closely tied to you for the rest of your life? Or are you willing to release him and to take this pain—all of your deep emotional wounds—and give everything to God?" A long pause followed as Philip carefully considered the implications. Then he replied, "I want to be rid of him." As God's grace flooded in, Philip earnestly prayed and emptied his anger bowl before the Lord.

In that moment, it was as if a cleansing flood of water washed over the raging fire within Philip's heart, dousing years of smoldering heartache. And, in that moment, he was free.

Finding What Fuels Your Anger

Philip's call clearly illustrates the kind of crippling confusion unresolved anger can create when we don't have a ready answer to the all-important question: Where does anger come from? For many people, any one of the fiery trials Philip faced would be more than sufficient to stoke the flames of fury.

Perhaps you recognize one or more of the four sources of anger in your own life. If so, there's no need to live in dread of the next spark or to feel helpless to prevent another raging inferno. Know what fuels your anger. Sift through and clean up the emotional debris in your life to forever stop harmful flare-ups.

God indeed hears our anguished cries and heals our hurting hearts. All we have to do is humble ourselves before Him...and ask. Trust in His infinite love and care and in His promise: "We know that in all things God works for the good of those who love him, who have been called according to his purpose" (Romans 8:28).

With regard to the cause of my father's abominable behavior, it was many years after his death that I learned some eye-opening information from one of his nephews. I always found it curious that my father spoke little of his family or childhood, but it never occurred to me to ask him or my mother about it. All I knew was that he left home in his early teens and never returned.

Because he was more than twice my mother's age when I was born,

I never knew his parents or siblings. I learned from his nephew that my paternal grandfather was extremely physically abusive, especially toward my father. On more than one occasion, my father sought refuge in the home of his older brother and spent numerous nights sleeping on a pew in a nearby church.

Needless to say, it was an "Aha!" moment for me. I felt a combination of sadness and relief. The mental imagery of any son being driven out of his home by an abusive father tore at my heartstrings. Now I had some understanding of his angry, hurtful ways. Hurt people... *hurt people.*

For the first time, I saw my father as a hurting little boy in a grown-up body. Although I had come to forgive him, at that moment I felt compassion for him welling up in me.

𖤣

How I thank God for caring enough about my healing journey to gift me with powerful insights into my father's past pain. Clearly, however, God is not finished with me yet.

4

Ashes to Ashes

The High Cost of Our Unresolved Anger

*"Hot-tempered people must pay the penalty.
If you rescue them once, you will have to do it again"*
(Proverbs 19:19 NLT).

IF BURNING ANGER came in a bottle, most people would want to bury it in the deepest hole at the most remote place on the planet—and seal it and label it with multiple warnings. We might stamp words like *explosive*, *volatile*, and *combustible* all over the bottle—or possibly *hot as blazes* and *active time bomb*—so people would dare not open it.

But rather than coming in a labeled bottle, anger shows up in various sizes, shapes, and shades often without warning.

Anger is a lot like the flame of a candle—it's associated with "heat" of varying degrees. Each hue of the flame is a different temperature, but no matter the blues, yellows, oranges, and reds, the one thing we all know is that the flame is *hot*—and if we put a finger into the flame we will get burned!

So it is with anger—there are varying degrees, and the higher the degree of heat, the deeper the degree of hurt. And even more so, the wider the area of hurt, the greater the destructive impact.

The book of Proverbs gives us this most graphic word picture: "Can a man scoop fire into his lap without his clothes being burned?"[1]

What a scene! Obviously fire in and of itself is not bad—a camp-fire is wonderful, but a "lap fire" is dreadful!

Let me be clear about this: Anger can be helpful, but anger that is misplaced and out of control can be horrible.

The Victims of Anger

Few of us intend to hurt others permanently—even when we are angry. We lash out, but hope there won't be any lingering effects. Few of us *want* to cause havoc and heartache for those around us. But the truth is, extreme anger is very much like a bomb—once it explodes, destruction is inevitable. It damages everything in its path, including relationships and reputations, people and professions, even property.

This isn't some abstract academic theory. By the time we reach adulthood, we've all seen it happen many times—on the playground, in the classroom, both at home and at work. Every time incendiary anger isn't snuffed out, the list of losses grows larger, the list of victims grows longer.

Counselors spend countless hours helping victims cope—the child of an angry parent, the spouse of an angry mate, or the target of an angry boss. Fortunately, with God's healing hand, those wounded by the flaming arrows of anger can move beyond *coping* to *healing*.

But it's just as important to remember the not-so-obvious victims of anger. I'm talking about the ones responsible for the emotional car-nage. When surveying the "scene of the crime," we divide ourselves into victims on one side and victimizers on the other. But our all-seeing, all-knowing God sees each heart in need of help and healing—the hurting hearts of both the abused and their abusers.

I believe that is how God saw my family—not five victims of one angry man, but six victims of anger. We all needed help and healing.

Proverbs 22:24-25 warns, "Do not make friends with a hot-tempered man, do not associate with one easily angered, or you may learn his ways and get yourself ensnared." God is telling us that rela-tionships with hot-tempered people always take a heavy toll—not just on those who are the target of rage, but also on those who feel powerless to stop the anger boiling up around them.

Plain and simple: You cannot stay around smoke without smelling like smoke. Likewise, you cannot stay around anger without taking on some characteristics of anger.

This principle was played out in my own life. My father's anger ignited my anger, which then resulted in anger controlling both of us. This is not the kind of healthy "sharing" God intends for dads and daughters. The very thing I hated in my dad took root in me, although I didn't see it at the time. Feeling totally justified in my anger, I didn't see any similarities between his anger and mine. I was right. He was wrong. But, in truth, we were both wrong. Neither of us allowed anger to accomplish good in us.

The High Price of Anger

Jesus said, "Each day has enough trouble of its own."[2] Life naturally brings us plenty of problems, and we can't afford to make matters worse with the horrific hardship of unrestrained rage. Let's examine six ways that we pay a high price for our anger:

1. Anger Destroys Relationships

"I want a divorce" was the last thing Rob expected to hear after returning home from a three-day Promise Keepers conference. But that evening Rob's wife, Judy, was unusually quiet. When he asked her why, her anguish poured out.

Judy explained that during the days Rob had been gone, a new sense of peace had settled over their household: "During the past three days, I've felt better about myself than I've ever felt during our marriage." Missing were his explosive outbursts of anger—and the anxiety they caused. For Rob, this painful moment of truth cut deeply.

Soon afterward, a marriage counselor identified the "pressure cooker" issue: Rob had a problem with unresolved anger that fueled his frequent rages. His verbal rantings had left Judy feeling wounded and fearful—not only for her own well-being, but for that of their young son, Tyler, as well.

Rob's reaction? "I got angry at the counselor!"

Several months later, unable to resolve their differences, the couple divorced. But by the grace of God, while Rob's marriage had ended, his journey of healing had just begun.

Uncontrolled anger is deadly to relationships because it undermines the very conditions necessary to create and maintain trust between people. Couples can ride out the storms of life together so long as trust rides with them, but unbridled anger destroys trust and makes the storms too threatening.

Healthy relationships require freedom from fear. To open our life to another person is, by definition, to make ourselves vulnerable. Like a fire victim being asked to jump from a rooftop above a raging inferno, we must be able to trust the one who says he is ready to catch us and break our fall.

If that person periodically lets go and we get hurt, the inevitable fear and uncertainty we feel will rob us of the strength and confidence we need to stay committed through tough times.

Random outbursts of raw anger can be terrifying. They create an environment in which everyone is guarded and ready to either fight or flee. This constant state of alertness saps vital trust, energy, and spontaneity from our lives. And its impact on our relationships? "Ashes to ashes"—utter devastation.

After his divorce—through circumstances only God could orchestrate—Rob met Jack, one of our enthusiastic Hope For The Heart team members. Learning of Jack's part in our ministry, Rob eagerly related how God had used Hope For The Heart to change his life. Humbled and inspired, Jack invited Rob to come to our weekly staff devotions. There, our team had the privilege of hearing the rest of Rob's story.

During a sleepless night a few months after his divorce, Rob turned on the radio. Our *Hope In The Night* radio program was airing, and the topic just happened to be anger. "I'd never heard the topic of anger approached from a biblical perspective. That broadcast was God-sent… no doubt about it."

Rob listened intently, then ordered our set of audio recordings and *Biblical Counseling Keys* on anger. With those in hand, he reserved an extended stay in a hotel room for a time of intense reading, listening, and praying. His goal was to grasp God's principles on dealing with his past anger and handling his present hostilities. Faithfully, God began to reveal the severity of Rob's problem.

"It hit me like a ton of bricks: I responded to people—especially my ex-wife—with rage, just erupting like a volcano." At 2:00 Sunday morning, Rob penned this journal entry: "Just like the eruption of a volcano, the hot lava pours down the mountain, scorching everything in sight. It changes the composition of the rock by its heat forever. Its damage is lasting and leaves black, ugly, scarred rock. My explosive anger scorches everyone in sight—my ex-wife, my son, my mother, employees—it scars them for life and leaves our relationships black and ugly. However, Christ can scrape away…scrape away the black outer covering through me as I forgive those who have made me angry and as I work to restore my relationships."

Rob said that over the next several months and years, "God gradually revealed to me the source of my anger, which was hurt and rejection from my childhood and teenage years. When I raged at Judy, I'd been trying to control her so she couldn't reject me. But in reality, I was making things worse."

Rob did the difficult work necessary to tame his toxic anger, and he continues to reap the rewards. His relationship with his son is blossoming in an atmosphere of trust and loving discipline. Though Judy has remarried, the two are now able to communicate openly so they can parent productively. In fact, Judy recently wrote Rob a letter, thanking him for his compassionate and Christlike attitude in the years following their divorce.

"I'm a work in progress," Rob told our team, concluding his inspirational visit. "I still get angry, but now I'm able to process my pain. Had it not been for your *Biblical Counseling Keys*, I wouldn't have changed. They brought healing through the application of God's Word. After years of burning others with my out-of-control anger, I finally know how to express my feelings constructively. Your ministry gave me the tools I needed. My dream now is to help others, along with their families, who are suffering just like I was."

2. Anger Destroys Harmony at Work

Anger and aggression in the workplace are increasing, making colleagues anything but congenial. This issue makes the evening news only when anger spawns horrible violence—which, sadly, is becoming increasingly commonplace.

But for many people, low-level frustration at work—simmering anger they feel themselves or must deal with in others—is a daily way of life that drains the workplace of the joy and satisfaction that a good day's work should bring. In fact, American companies spend billions of dollars on legal fees, medical expenses, lost employee time, and related expenses every year dealing with the consequences of workplace anger that turns violent.[3]

Yet even without physical aggression, unresolved anger among employees diminishes productivity, inhibits creativity, and limits personal success. Left unchecked, it usually costs the angry person both a good job and good references, not to mention the loss of potentially meaningful work relationships. Managers and corporate bosses certainly don't want their company to be the next to make headlines because they allowed a conflict to turn ugly.

Dave is a good example. This retired military man—now in his second career—became a project manager at a prominent software design company. His job was to oversee the development of a new program that would help streamline accounting tasks for small businesses. He had a staff of 20 programmers working around the clock, but as the project deadline approached, it became increasingly clear something was wrong. The software failed every important test run, and each attempted correction only made things worse.

When senior managers decided it was time to take a closer look, it didn't take long to identify the trouble: Staff communication and trust had been completely broken. The troubleshooting process of pinpointing problems and solving them as a team had ceased to function. The programmers were afraid to report glitches and failures—a necessary part of testing and improving the product.

It turned out that when they did speak up, Dave often exploded in a terrible rage. By shouting put-downs and slamming doors, he made it clear he would not tolerate bad news. So his employees stopped giving it to him...with disastrous results.

Dave was a smart, competent man. But he was used to giving orders to soldiers and pushing for the results he wanted, no matter what. The corporate model of consensus and team building didn't make sense to him. As a result, he mistakenly saw every problem as a breakdown of "discipline" that needed to be quashed.

The more Dave's management style failed, the angrier he became. And the angrier he became, the more his management style failed. It was a downward spiral that repeated itself again and again when anger gained the upper hand. Eventually, the company had no choice but to replace Dave with someone more skilled in communication and problem-solving...and less likely to erupt in anger.

Dave's story brings to mind a therapeutic camping program for troubled youth, where a close friend of mine worked. Three counselors would take 10 teens camping in the wilderness for 26 days at a stretch. The goal: to teach them how to talk their problems out rather than fight them out or run away from them.

Needless to say, problems were easy to come by in the hot, dry Chihuahuan Desert of southwest Texas. And there was definitely no place to run away to. Before leaving Dallas, by prior agreement with all 10 teens, when tempers flared, everything came to a screeching halt.

No one could fix a meal, hike to water, go to sleep—not until the problem was resolved.

Immediately the group would circle together (called a "huddle up") to clarify the problem and come up with a workable solution—agreeable not only to the parties involved, but to the *entire group*. Then it was back to the challenge of climbing mountains and surviving in the desert. It's amazing how quickly hot tempers cool down when the stakes are high enough—such as eating!

> Your health is powerfully affected by what you think and feel.

Dave's story might have had a different ending if he had been confronted sooner about his angry, demoralizing management style, but instead, both a project and a job were sacrificed.

Let's face it: Work can be very stressful. Many people feel pressured by deadlines, bullied by bosses, frustrated by missed promotions, and impatient with underachieving coworkers or demanding clients. But allowing anger to boil over into intimidating outbursts not only makes things worse, it offers no help to everyone involved.

As in Dave's case, excessive anger can result in unemployment—which then can be added to the list of reasons to be angry. Who can afford that kind of costly anger?

And what society can long survive such destructive behavior? That's why God's Word says, "Refrain from anger and turn from wrath; do not fret—it leads only to evil. For evil men will be cut off."[4]

3. Anger Destroys Our Health

One of the most intriguing ideas to emerge in medical science is also the most often ignored. In its simplest form: Your health is powerfully affected by what you think and feel. This fact is presented throughout the Bible, and today, there are those in medical science who "get it."

The traditional belief held is that good health depends only on external factors such as rest, nutrition, and exercise. Yet when it comes to health, in truth, intangible influences are powerfully at work as well. Researchers have discovered that our thoughts directly affect the creation of real biochemical compounds—such as adrenaline and endorphins—which have a significant impact on how our bodies function.

Here's a simple demonstration: Imagine you've just come home from the grocery store with a carton full of ripe, plump strawberries (or your favorite fruit). You can't wait to take a bite and slowly savor the sweetness on your taste buds. You wish you could savor that succulent flavor forever.

If you are like me, your mouth is watering in anticipation as you read these words. Why? The beautiful, delectable fruit exists only in your mind as a thought, but your body reacts nonetheless with a very real physical response. This happens frequently, whether you are aware of it or not. Many thoughts and emotions have a tangible effect on our bodies, and anger is one of the most potent.

Dr. Redford Williams, director of the Behavioral Medicine Research Center at Duke University, has spent much of his career studying the effects of sustained hostility on the human body. He says:

> There is some evidence that the immune system may be weaker in hostile people. According to a study of more than 1,000 people at a Western Electric factory in Chicago over a 25-year period, those with high hostility scores were at a high risk of dying not only from coronary disease but from cancer as well.[5]

In other words, living in a constant state of angry frustration is physically harmful. In fact, *it can kill you*. Here are some findings from similar studies:

- According to the American College of Cardiology, sudden cardiac death accounts for 400,000 deaths each year in the United States.
- In 2009, a group from Yale University studied 62 patients with heart disease and implantable defibrillators that detect dangerous heart arrhythmias and deliver an electrical shock

to restore a normal heartbeat. The subjects were put through an exercise in which the patient recounted a recent angry episode while the electrical activity of the heart was measured. The study found that *anger increased electrical instability* in these patients. The study followed these patients for three years and suggests that anger impacts the heart's electrical system *in ways that can lead to sudden death.*[6]

- A study of men found those "generally hostile and contemptuous of other people" are *30 percent more likely to develop a heart condition* called atrial fibrillation—a "flutter" that signals an *increased risk of stroke.*[7]

- Increased heart rate and blood pressure when a person is angry cause "micro-tears" in the lining of the arteries, making it *easier for blockages to form.*[8]

- A study begun in 1983 concluded that medical students with high "hostility" levels while in school were *seven times more likely to die before age 50*—of any cause—than their calmer peers.[9]

- People who already suffer from heart disease nearly *triple their risk of a heart attack* when they become extremely angry. The increased vulnerability lasts for at least two hours.[10]

- A survey of nearly 2500 emergency room patients who had been injured in some way found that "people who described themselves as feeling irritable have a 30% increased risk for getting injured, while those who are feeling hostile *double their risk of injury.*"[11]

Researchers acknowledge there are many factors that contribute to ill health, and it is increasingly clear an angry disposition is one of them. Psychologist Ernest Johnson put it this way: "In the end, for many people who have problems really expressing and dealing with their feelings, there's early mortality—dropping dead from a stroke or a heart attack, kidney disease or breast cancer."[12]

It's hard to get any more blunt than that. No wonder God tells us to guard our hearts and our minds and to give careful thought to our ways. And no wonder He warns us regarding anger and angry people.

The Bible says, "Everyone should be quick to listen, slow to speak and slow to become angry, for man's anger does not bring about the righteous life that God desires."[13]

4. Anger Causes Irrational Thinking

When people get angry, their problem-solving ability plummets. Consider the case of my normally even-keeled assistant, Elizabeth, who recently shared this story with those attending our monthly *Biblical Counseling Institute*.

"Many years ago, I was driving to a corporate planning conference where I was to serve as a presenter for the opening session. Hoping to arrive early, I instead became ensnarled in a terrible traffic jam. With each passing minute, I became more frantic.

"My hands gripped the steering wheel...my jaw tightened...I could hardly take my eyes off the clock on the car dashboard. My heart raced as I scanned the horizon looking for a way—any way—to escape the gridlock. I began tailgating. Soon I was eyeing the median, wondering if I could somehow sail across it in the family minivan and find another route."

As her anxiety mounted, Elizabeth had no way of knowing that important chemical changes were also taking place inside her body. Here's what happens when circumstances stress us:

- Epinephrine (adrenaline) is released by the adrenal glands,[14] immediately preparing the body for a fight-or-flight response. However, if fight or flight does not occur, the highly energized body has difficulty calming down. (This is why angry people experience a racing heart, shaking hands, and fast breathing.)

- The angry person's hormones then travel from the brain to

the adrenal glands, signaling the need for tension reduction by the release of cortisol. However, cortisol raises blood pressure above the norm, which makes *rational thinking more difficult.*

Elizabeth continued her story:

"As I sat there stewing, the thought crossed my mind that I had done everything but pray and give thanks to God in my situation. I realized the Bible says, 'Do not be anxious about anything, but in everything, by prayer and petition, with thanksgiving, present your requests to God.'[15] However, I was so anxious I could barely comprehend the thought. But still it persisted. So in a very sarcastic, very loud voice, I blurted out, 'Okay, God, *thank You*! Sitting in this traffic jam…being late for the big conference…is *just great*! I mean I'm *really thankful*, God. In fact, if I were any more thankful, I just don't know what I'd do!'

"Just hearing myself be so irreverent, angry, and sarcastic with my wonderful, loving, patient heavenly Father jolted me. I felt convicted and saddened by my disrespectful attitude. After a minute or two, my heart began to soften and I began, again, to talk to God: 'Lord, I'm sorry I have such a terrible attitude…that I'm so impatient and angry. I commit this drive and this day to You. Thank You for waking me up this morning…for giving me a car to drive and a job to drive it to. Thank You for taking such good care of me. Thank You that I'm not the one involved in the accident that's slowing us down this morning. Please help those involved in the crash. I trust this drive to You and ask You to get me to the conference in Your perfect time. I love You, Lord! Amen.'

"Unexplainable peace seemed to envelop every square inch of my car. It's like I was driving a joy bubble. Instead of feeling anxious and angry, I felt calm and at perfect ease. I relaxed, sat back, and drove safely. I even began to sing. The traffic began to open up, and I arrived at the meeting in time to start my presentation."

This really should come as no surprise to us because after we do what the Bible says—sincerely pray about our problems with thanks-giving—then we receive what is described in the very next verse: "And the peace of God, which transcends all understanding, will guard your hearts and your minds in Christ Jesus."[16]

5. Anger Undermines Mental and Emotional Well-Being

There is a big difference between occasionally getting angry and being an angry person. Getting angry when circumstances call for it is a natural response, whereas being angry most of the time is a precursor to a psychological enemy that stalks millions of people: chronic depression.

In fact, numerous studies confirm anger and depression go hand in hand, particularly when we get angry with ourselves.

What a sad and self-destructive price we pay for anger. The truth is that anger and depression feed each other in a relentless downward spiral of despair. The angrier you become, the more depressed you feel. The deeper you sink into depression, the angrier you feel.

Fortunately, God has provided a way to deliver us from this double dose of pain. Jesus said, "Come to me, all you who are weary and burdened, and I will give you rest. Take my yoke upon you and learn from me, for I am gentle and humble in heart."[17] What do we learn from what Jesus has modeled for us? To let go and to forgive.

The evidence is clear: Unresolved anger is toxic to the human heart, mind, and body. To live the life God intended, your anger simply *must* be poured out into the Refiner's fire. Allow God to burn away the damaging dross that has accumulated from years of anger, resentment, and bitterness.

6. Anger Hinders Our Christian Walk

God gives you permission to be angry. He never says, "Thou shalt not ever be angry!" He made you in such a way that expressing anger is a natural, spontaneous part of being human—like laughing or crying. What He does say is don't sin and don't *stay* angry. Specifically, "'In your anger do not sin': Do not let the sun go down while you are still angry, and do not give the devil a foothold."[18]

Why is it important to resolve anger before you lay your head down at night? What opportunity does prolonged anger give the enemy of our souls? And just how does nursing hostility leave the door open for evil to creep in on us?

Imagine you are visiting the home of a dear friend. You both look forward to an evening of laughter and conversation. In the living room is a fireplace with a raging fire.

The fire is too hot for the small room, and right away, you start to sweat. It's hard to breathe. You move your chair as far from the flames as you are able, but before long you can't focus on a single word your friend is saying. All you can think about is that fire and how uncomfortable you are.

That's exactly what raging anger does to our relationship with God—it *dominates*, while our spiritual vitality *diminishes*. As long as our anger burns, it's next to impossible for us to concentrate on anything else. Our anger bowls impede our view as we attempt to journey in our walk of faith.

The Christlike walk comprises in part love, forgiveness, humility, and prayerfulness. There is no place for unresolved anger in the mix. Here are three reasons why:

- *Anger suffocates our motivation to love our enemies.* It is okay to be angry—on our way to forgiving our offender. Unresolved anger drives us toward revenge, not reconciliation—toward hatred, not love. Jesus unequivocally says, "Love your enemies" (Matthew 5:44). (This is not emotional love. The Greek term Matthew 5:44 uses for love is *agape*, which refers to a commitment to doing what is best for the other person.)

- *Anger smothers our motivation to pray for our enemies.* The longer we fume over an offense, the harder it will be to pray for those who have hurt us. In fact, typically the last person we want to pray for is the one who has hurt us. Yet Jesus, who understands your anger, says, "Pray for those who persecute you."[19]

- *Anger stifles our motivation to surrender to God's will.* Rage is an attempt to control the people and events in our lives and make them bend to *our* desires. It's necessary to tame the flames before you can expect to sincerely say to God, "Not my will, but yours" (Luke 22:42).

What is God's will? Even when we've been unjustly wronged, Jesus commands us to forgive and to cancel the offender's debt, just as our debts have been wiped clean by the Savior. The Bible says, "Love for God" is "to obey his commands."[20] Don't allow anger to drive a wedge between you and your love for God.

⚜

So the bad news is…chronic anger is costly, taking a tremendous toll on our physical, emotional, and spiritual well-being. It contains the power to ruin our relationships, impair our employment, damage our health, and interfere with our walk with God. And that's just the short list.

The good news is…we are not doomed to a lifetime of lament. The Bible says, "If anyone is in Christ, he is a new creation; the old has gone, the new has come!"[21]

If you are in Christ, you are a new creation. This means the past is wiped clean. God has made this possible, and He makes it possible— "as far as it depends on you"[22]—to know peace, healing, and hope in all your relationships and circumstances.

The Fire Eaters

The Harm of Holding In Our Anger

"Careful words make for a careful life; careless talk may ruin everything"
(PROVERBS 13:3 MSG).

SO THAT'LL BE a cheeseburger—hold the onions—one large order of fries, and a supersized bowl of anger. Anything else?"

Had a restaurant server attempted to confirm such an order in my younger years, I would have quickly corrected him. *Never* would it have been my intent to down a big, steaming bowl of fiery anger. But for a number of years, anger had become a staple in my emotional diet.

Growing up in an unpredictable home that fostered anger, I frequently chose silence when fiery eruptions occurred. Going underground with my feelings seemed the only way to survive in the presence of my painfully punitive father, who tolerated *no anger* but his own.

"Eating" my anger felt less dangerous than allowing it to surface. But over time, I've learned that when we submerge anger, it's only a matter of time before it comes raging back to the surface—hotter and more harmful. I was subconsciously heaping my hurts into an anger bowl that seemed to resemble a bottomless pit. But every bowl has a bottom; not a single slip of paper denoting an angry incident just "disappeared."

Fear Evokes Fire Eating

If you consistently internalize your anger, it doesn't take a rocket scientist to figure out why—the reason is *fear*. Either you're afraid of what *you* will do if you express your feelings, or you fear what *others* will do (as in my case).

I constantly evaluated my situation: What will it cost me to be candid, to be honest? Security? Safety? Survival? I didn't risk showing anger without calculating my potential losses. And from my fear-based perspective, the cost seemed to always exceed the gain.

Unfortunately, when fear is the dominant decision maker, the idea that you might gain something by expressing your anger appropriately never enters the equation. Soon, you conclude it's *always* safer to just "stuff it."

That may sound cowardly, but in truth, many of us "anger eaters" have had good reasons to run from conflict. To survive we've had to find a way to endure relationships characterized by anger. Once in place, these patterns of behavior become reflexive, a kind of subconscious survival instinct that governs our relationships from then on.

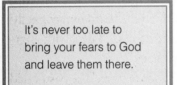

It's never too late to bring your fears to God and leave them there.

Realize that whether you detonate your anger in public or swallow it in private, you will end up scorched—and possibly scarred for life. Anger must be dealt with, period. The good news is that it's a comprehensive exercise that leads to incredible relief and freedom, and it's an exercise that we don't have to undertake on our own. How comforting that the Lord says, "Do not fear, for I am with you; do not be dismayed, for I am your God. I will strengthen you and help you; I will uphold you with my righteous right hand" (Isaiah 41:10).

The Six Kinds of Anger Eaters

There are many ways to avoid confronting your anger. They run the gamut from total denial to clandestine counterattacks. That is why honestly identifying *your approach* is a great place to begin getting control over the smoldering and sometimes blazing fires within. Consider these common types of *anger avoiders* and see if you recognize yourself:

1. Stuffers: "Who, me? Angry?"

Everyone who knew Joan marveled that she seemed completely unflappable. She never raised her voice or lost her composure, even when tempers flared all around her. In her position as the office manager of a large church, Joan's restraint served her well.

Coordinating the activities of eight full-time pastors and a dozen other staff members was enough to challenge anyone. But not Joan. She was calm and competent beyond belief. A prominent church member once joked that if Joan had worked for Moses, she'd have served Pharaoh tea and cookies and had the children of Israel peacefully on their way before lunch.

It was a reputation Joan enjoyed and cultivated. Imagine her surprise, then, when the senior pastor began a private meeting with her by asking a startling question.

"Joan," he said, "I wonder if you'd be willing to share with me why you are so angry?" She was floored. What? Had she heard him correctly?

"But I'm not angry," she said with a serene smile. "I deal with angry people all the time, but I'm never one of them."

"I'll agree with you that you never lose your temper," the pastor said. "But that isn't the same thing as not being angry." Having observed Joan at work, the pastor noticed a formidable line of emotional defenses just beneath the surface of her even-keel demeanor that kept everyone at a safe distance.

True, no one got under her skin enough to provoke her anger. But neither did they get close enough to enjoy her friendship or trust. Furthermore, he noticed her placid approach to life masked the harsh, punitive core of high standards she set for her subordinates.

Stuffers are people who hide their anger well. They are fearful of its negative consequences. They convince themselves—and sometimes others—that it never existed in the first place. They stuff it down inside, hoping to forget all about it, like the slightly smoldering firecracker relegated to the bottom of the fireworks box. Out of sight, out of mind... *for a while.*

On the surface, the strategy appears to work just fine. Like Joan, these folks often project a soft, magnanimous personality in public—even when enduring a painful offense that would infuriate most people. They simply smile and get on with life as if nothing is wrong.

But anger exists for a reason and doesn't just disappear because you tell it to. Anger tells *you* when something needs your attention. Ignoring it doesn't make it go away. No matter how deeply you hide your anger—even from yourself—it will eventually make its way back to the surface of your life, often with a vengeance.

Joan left her pastor's office that day truly baffled. But she took his gentle suggestion that she ask God to show her any hidden anger she might secretly harbor. She went home and adopted David's prayer in Psalm 139:23-24:

> *"Search me, O God, and know my heart;*
> *test me and know my anxious thoughts.*
> *See if there is any offensive way in me,*
> *and lead me in the way everlasting."*

It didn't take long for Joan to find an answer—she had, indeed, deeply entrenched anger. Instead of releasing her anger to God, she had been harboring her anger...toward God.

Ten years earlier, Joan and her husband tragically lost their first baby to a rare kind of respiratory infection. Joan had never resolved her bitter rage at God for allowing the tragedy to strike her family. At the time, Joan was devastated and so overwhelmed with grief that denial shielded her thoughts like an iron curtain, holding back raw emotion and all hope of healing.

Now, upon prayer and reflection, Joan realized her pastor was right. In spite of her determined denial, the heat of hidden anger had silently seared her relationships all these years. Freedom came as she prayerfully acknowledged each hurt, and then gratefully released them all to God.

If you are a "stuffer" and want to be free, take heart. Nothing is hidden so deeply that God can't reach down and make it right. I know because He reached into the depths of my being, uprooted the bitterness, and extinguished the anger burning toward my father. Be assured He can and wants to do the same for you.

2. Sulkers: "Just leave me alone."

Unlike Joan, some people know very well they are angry, but have no intention of risking more pain and hardship by confronting their issues head-on. Rather than deny their anger, they simply pull down the shades of their heart and hang a "Do Not Disturb" sign on the door. From within this sullen fortress they resist all attempts from others to confront their anger and resolve it. The very last thing they want to do is *talk* about it.

Clearly, we all deserve privacy and the right to deal with anger in our own way. But sulkers usually aren't just taking a time-out, or pausing to count to ten before proceeding. These are people who completely withdraw from relationships and can nurse a grudge in silence for *years*. Sadly, they allow a past wrong to burn up any prospect for joy in the present and to destroy any hope for joy in the future.

Withdrawing is a breeding ground for bitterness that is practically guaranteed to inflame your anger, not tame it. Cut off from other points of view, you are much more susceptible to error and exaggeration in your thinking. In your mind, you replay the anger-producing offense again and again until it grows out of proportion.

Living with a Turtle

Lee wanted his wife's forgiveness. Uncharacteristically, he'd had too much to drink at Jana's office Christmas party and became overly loud and obnoxious. To make matters worse, he blatantly flirted with two of his wife's coworkers. When Jana told him it was time to go, he said he was sick of her "mothering."

The next day, Lee was horrified at his own despicable behavior. He was desperate to communicate how sorry he was and to begin repairing the damage done. There was just one problem: Jana refused to listen to what he had to say or even share her feelings about what had happened. Obviously humiliated and embarrassed, she wore her hurt like a suit of armor and withdrew behind its cold, hard exterior.

You see, Jana's grandfather was an alcoholic with a long history of ruining family events, especially holidays, by drinking too much. Lee's behavior struck a tender nerve in Jana's heart. She responded to her fear and anger the same way her mother and grandmother had: She retreated to a "safe distance" and silently fumed. Her anger was plain to see, but completely inaccessible.

By the time Lee called me on *Hope In The Night*, he was desperate to break through the firewall of Jana's closed-off emotions. "She's a turtle. She pulls her head inside her shell and won't come out. There's absolutely nothing I can do or say!"

"Lee, I hear your frustration. Sulking keeps anger alive by slamming the door on honest, direct communication. Yet communication is the essential ingredient of eventual forgiveness and reconciliation. Sulking denies passage even to the most sincere apology. It's one of the behaviors the apostle Paul had in mind when he wrote: 'Do not let the sun go down while you are still angry, and do not give the devil a foothold.'[1]

"You already know you can't *force* Jana to open up. But I believe there are steps you can take to strengthen your relationship with your wife. Would you be willing to explore what *you* can do in this situation and forget, at least for a moment, what you want *her* to do?"

Refocus on What Can Be Controlled

Lee seemed skeptical, but agreed to hear me out, enabling me to direct his attention to what he could control. Since Jana's trust had been violated, reconciliation would require time, a behavior change, and consistency to prove to Jana that Lee was worthy of her trust. He could not expect her to re-extend trust without his demonstration of a true understanding of what he had done wrong, how deeply it had hurt her, a godly sorrow over his actions, and sincere repentance.

I probed Lee's decision to drink too much at the party and to make passes at Jana's colleagues. It became clear that Lee had deficits in his own life that would require his focused attention.

"Lee, I'm going to recommend you involve a godly man, or even two or three, in your life—to provide support, prayer, and accountability on your journey toward reconciliation. Is there anyone in your life who could come alongside you?"

"I know one man who is a really strong Christian. I could ask if he'd be willing to help me."

Develop a Dialogue of Integrity

"Good! Ask him. And in the meantime, I'm going to recommend some things you can say when you talk to Jana about this issue. Of course, these words won't do you a bit of good unless they come from your heart. But if you can say this and mean it, consider communicating something along these lines:

"'Jana, my actions at the party were completely wrong—I have no excuse. And I realize I opened up that old wound from your grandfather when I got out of control. I acted like him.

"'I know you are feeling hurt, betrayed, embarrassed, and fearful. And I don't blame you one bit. I pray that someday you'll forgive me. But I know I can't demand your forgiveness...and I must earn your trust. That's what I want to do, no matter how long it takes.'"

Because Lee had committed his life to Christ, he needed to tell her that and state, "With God's help, I am going to do everything I can to become a man of integrity. As a Christian, that's my deepest desire. And as my wife, that's what you deserve."

Over the years, many men (and women) in Lee's situation—people who had "blown it" and then had to face the consequence of living with a sulker—have contacted me with glowing reports of restoration. But they had to take the necessary steps to address their *own* issues and live a life of total integrity before their loved ones.

3. Snipers: "Can you believe what she did to me?"

While some people hide behind an impenetrable shield of silence, others are more than willing to talk about their anger—to everyone except the person who sparked it. They avoid owning up to their rage by diverting its energy into making sure everyone knows their version of events.

The payoff in using this approach is twofold. First, in playing the aggrieved victim, why do the strenuous work of resolving the conflict when you can bask in an outpouring of pity instead? Don't misunderstand me—we all appreciate genuine compassion when a painful event has caused us harm. That's a natural and healthy role friends and family can play in our lives. The problem arises when we begin to crave the "camaraderie" inspired by our anger—so much so that we stay stuck there.

Second, by engaging in gossip about the people who made them mad, snipers often succeed in *imparting* their anger to others— empowering them to also fire their angry bullets. Shared anger means shared responsibility for action. In this way, they enlist surrogates willing to take the lead in confronting the "offender" on their behalf. In other words, the snipers' fear of anger leads them to create a human shield around themselves, something they hide behind for as long as they're able to keep the collective fire hot.

When you are angry, don't hesitate to call on the support of wise friends. But remember that your anger is *yours*, and solidarity with others is a stepping-stone toward receiving God's gift of freedom and healing—not a destination in itself.

4. Schemers: "I never get mad—I just get even."

Recently I heard about a husband who questioned his wife, "How can you be so calm when I lose my temper so much?" She answered, "I clean the toilet." Still confused, he asked, "Well, how does that help?" She replied demurely, "I use your toothbrush."

A humorous story, perhaps, but real-life anger issues aren't quite so laughable.

Shirley was already angry with her husband, Neil. She had felt for some time that she did far more than her share to keep their household running smoothly. Both had demanding jobs that contributed income to the family. But when it came to doing the laundry, making dinner, cleaning the bathrooms, or getting the kids to bed on time, the responsibility wasn't distributed evenly. There seemed to be an unspoken assumption that *all* those responsibilities belonged *only* to her.

"At times I felt guilty for being irritated," Shirley told me. "An image would pop into my head of my mother—the perfect, happy homemaker. She never complained or got angry about all she did for us. So neither should I."

But when Neil announced he had joined a fitness center and planned to work out for an hour a couple of evenings a week, it was too much for Shirley. She became furious. Couldn't Neil see she was already stretched to the breaking point? Of course, that would have been a perfect time for Shirley to openly confront her anger, but that's not what she did. She was unable to escape the memory of her mother's voice saying, "God can't hear you when you grumble, dear."

So, instead of acting on her anger directly, Shirley channeled it into a series of less risky hit-and-run attacks—a campaign of emotional guerrilla warfare. She intentionally "forgot" to include Neil's clothes in the laundry one week. She fed the kids early some nights and told Neil to "fend for himself" with leftovers. She went shopping and spent more than usual on new clothes for herself. The problem was, none of these actions eased her anger. The more she got even, the worse she felt. "Then Neil started getting angry, too, but not knowing *why* I was behaving the way I was," she said.

Cultivate Clear, Credible Communication

"Shirley, you haven't been candid with Neil. Is it possible you are expecting him to read your mind?" I asked when we spoke on *Hope In The Night*.

"He's a smart man. Shouldn't he be able to figure out something so obvious? We've been married for twelve years. This doesn't take a mind reader."

"But only *you* know what's in your head and heart. True communication occurs when there is *shared understanding*. It's a process of revealing our values, assumptions, beliefs, and expectations.[2] It involves listening, clarifying, and many other important tasks. Deep, meaningful communication doesn't just happen. It takes work. Let me ask: So far, what's been the result of assuming Neil should *simply know* how you're feeling?"

"I've been wrong."

"Shirley, have you ever heard that great Albert Einstein quote: 'Insanity is doing the same thing over and over again and expecting different results'?"[3]

"Now *that's* funny! I use that line with my kids all the time."

"Could it also apply to the way you and Neil are attempting to communicate with each other?"

"The way we've been living since Neil joined the gym has me tied up in knots."

"Well I've got some good news for you. You can begin today to untie those knots—the ones in your heart and the ones in your marriage. Would you be willing to set aside some time this weekend to talk to Neil...to tell him how you're feeling, and share your heart with him? Even if you have some fear of his response, it is the truth, and speaking the truth in love sets you free! Are you ready to make that investment in your marriage?"

The Sandwich Technique

"I'm seeing that, to turn our marriage around, I probably have no other choice." Thankfully, Shirley decided to face her fears about openly communicating with her husband. Heartened by her courageous decision, I encouraged her to ask for what she needed emotionally from Neil. I also suggested she position any criti-

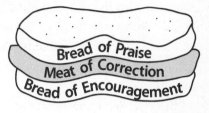

cism as though it were a piece of meat in the middle of a sandwich. That is, to "sandwich" the "meat of correction" between the "bread of praise" (a positive statement about Neil, a sincere compliment, or statement of genuine care) and the "bread of encouragement" (a statement expressing Shirley's confidence and assurance of the future success of their marriage).

After Shirley and Neil had their talk, things improved dramatically. He saw her point of view and agreed to make appropriate changes in his behavior—like sharing some of the responsibilities at home. Likewise, she continued practicing her new communication skills. Rather than scheming to get even when Neil disappointed her, Shirley gradually began to feel better about herself—and her marriage.

When God said, "It is mine to avenge; I will repay,"[4] His purpose was not to reserve for Himself the pleasure of getting even. He was warning us to avoid the perils of letting our anger lead to a destructive escalation of conflict. If you've handled anger by scheming ways to get back at someone, try God's plan for a change: "Do not repay anyone evil for evil."[5] Rather, give God your bowl of vengeful anger and let His healing comfort fill your heart.

5. Sweeteners: "Thanks for being there...when I needed you here!"

The writer of Proverbs tells us, "A gentle answer turns away wrath."[6] That is certainly true. But have you ever noticed that a gentle answer can also be used to *conceal* wrath? That a compliment can become a weapon?

For years, my nonconfrontational mother would say, "If you can't

say something nice, don't say anything at all." Well, in truth sweeteners are anger-avoiders who have rewritten the adage to read, "If you
can't bring yourself to say what's
really bothering you, say something 'nice' instead."

> Let anger serve its rightful purpose of drawing attention to a problem that needs to be solved.

Trying to be nice when you
are really feeling angry is like
camouflaging a time bomb with
ribbons and bows.

It looks pretty enough, and people on the receiving end have a
hard time turning it down. But, in truth, the disguised explosive is
meant not to delight, but to punish and wound. It is a sneaky way to
lash out at someone who has made you angry while hiding behind a
shield of plausible denial.

A sweetener will say, "You did a good job" when he is thinking,
You should have known not to do it this way!

Or, she will say, "I appreciate your help so much" when she is thinking, *I can't believe you handled it that way!*

Here's the bottom line: A bomb with a pretty bow on top is still
a bomb. Sooner or later, you'll have to quit passing it off as a present
and either detonate or diffuse it (that is, blow up because of it or honestly talk about it). Chances are, those with whom you are in conflict
aren't fooled anyway. Why not be honest from the beginning? Why
not let anger serve its rightful purpose of drawing attention to a problem that needs to be solved, rather than creating another problem to
pile on top of the existing one?

6. Self-blamers: "It's all my fault."

Counselors who work with victims of domestic violence for any
length of time get used to hearing them say, "I brought it on myself.
If only I hadn't…" Just fill in the blank with any number of perceived
failings on the part of the abused as justification for the actions of their
abusers. These victims invent endless variations of gray in any situation,

whereas emotionally healthy people will clearly see the stark black and white—the obvious right from wrong. And victims blame themselves rather than risk facing the fact that they are in a troubled, abusive relationship. For them, the truth must be avoided at almost all costs.

Some anger-avoiders operate the same way, even without the threat of physical violence. For them it feels far safer to plead guilty for sparking a conflict than to ever utter the words, "You hurt me. I am angry."

These overly submissive self-blamers have been emotionally battered by angry, controlling people who consistently find ways to successfully transfer their fault onto others. Therefore, the names in the anger bowls of the self-blamers are their *own*. After repeatedly being falsely accused and repeatedly failing to "win" their case, *Why not save a step, avoid a fight, and just succumb to the inevitable?* reasons the self-blamer.

I personally know about this type of anger-avoider. For years, it seemed smarter to give in than to fight a losing battle. After all, I found that acquiescing (and sometimes admitting guilt—falsely) ended the conflict sooner and momentarily appeased my accuser. Plus, it prompted peace—but not peace within me, and not peace with God.

The truth is, taking blame that doesn't belong to you can lead to all sorts of self-destructive beliefs and behaviors. Your anger is still there, sending the message that "there is something wrong." However, you've come to believe that what's wrong is *you*.

Self-blamers label themselves as guilty, stupid, foolish, and worthless. The distorted assumptions result in low self-worth, self-rejection, and false guilt. And it can lead to eating disorders, drug and alcohol abuse, sex and pornography addictions, dependence on antidepressants, and even suicide. In other words, blaming yourself to avoid your anger—or someone else's—is wrought with self-destructive tendencies.

When something happens to make you angry, do you find yourself fanning the flame of self-blame? If so, find healing for your seared emotions through the power of God's Word:

> *"Who will bring any charge against those whom God has chosen?*
> *It is God who justifies. Who is he that condemns? Christ Jesus,*

> *who died—more than that, who was raised to life—is at the*
> *right hand of God and is also interceding for us."*[7]

If the Son of God Himself doesn't condemn you, then surely it is safe to face your anger without condemning yourself. Take it to Him for wisdom and guidance.

Once I began to see the destructive effects of self-blaming, I diligently searched the Scriptures to find out how God sees me, and then learned to line up my thinking with His. I came to understand my worth and value to Jesus and to trust His Spirit within me to use the gifts He had given me to accomplish His purpose for me.

※

There are many ways to avoid facing your anger—but absolutely no good reasons for doing so. Anger is energy meant to flow through us like electricity turning the motor of positive change in our lives. Sometimes it forces us to look honestly at ourselves and admit where we need work. At other times, the message is that it's okay to stand up to unjust treatment in our relationships and to stop being a doormat for angry people.

With the powerful help of the Lord, you can learn to address, not avoid, anger in your life. Let's face it—fire eating is far from satisfying!

The Flamethrowers

The Damaging Displays of Our Anger

"Short-tempered people do foolish things."
(PROVERBS 14:17 NLT)

HE WAS CAUTIONED...counseled...commanded. He was more than well aware of the danger. He received repeated instructions to leave as Mount St. Helens quivered and quaked. But 84-year-old Harry Truman stood his ground near the volatile volcano.[1]

As the shifts beneath the earth's surface were regularly recorded—seismic activity logged day after day—Harry repeatedly turned a deaf ear to evacuation orders. He had gained quite a reputation over the years for holding out when everyone else was heading out.

The former bootlegger had left his rebellious life of running Canadian whiskey to California during the Prohibition years, but there was still plenty of rebel left in him. Harry wasn't about to budge from his lodge near Spirit Lake in Washington State. In 1929, he staked a 40-acre claim. And in the spring of 1980, he staked his life.

Known as a cantankerous wilderness guide—as rough and rugged as they come—Harry had already withstood 100-mile-an-hour windstorms, a fire that engulfed his house, and numerous earthquakes. If the volcano should start spewing out lava, Harry assumed he would have enough time to escape into an old mine shaft he had stocked with food and whiskey.

Despite ongoing eruptions of steam, harmonic tremors, and even a summit explosion, bullheaded Harry refused to budge. Although the number of eruptions lessened through March and April, the evacuation mandates continued.

Harry Truman's tenacity mirrored that of his presidential namesake. He once quipped, "If you can't stand the heat, you better get out of the kitchen!"[2] As conditions eventually worsened in the vicinity of the volcano, most people did "get out of the kitchen"—but not tough ole Harry.

In fact, Harry gained national notoriety after a Portland, Oregon, television station interviewed him. Reporters from one news show even visited him via helicopter. Harry could literally have been lifted out of harm's way, but he remained unwilling to leave.

Years ago I remember reading about "Holdout Harry" in the newspaper. I also remember seeing the televised interviews featuring his overconfident bravado: "I'm gonna stay right here…I've stuck it out 54 years and I can stick it out another 54!"[3]

On May 18, 1980, a 5.0 magnitude earthquake sent a blistering ash cloud up in the air—a blast clocked at 300 miles per hour. The powerful eruption triggered an avalanche of devastating, fiery debris—the largest ever recorded at that time.[4] That fateful day, 57 people lost their lives—including Harry, who was buried deep beneath a massive flow of ash and lava.

Evacuate Before the Volcano Erupts

Like live volcanoes, hot-tempered people steam and stew below the surface. When the inner pressure builds to the boiling point, their rage explodes—burning and scarring those around them like molten lava. They vent their volcanic wrath and cause widespread devastation.

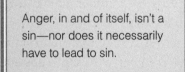

Anger, in and of itself, isn't a sin—nor does it necessarily have to lead to sin.

As I've thought about the volcanic people in my life, I've wished I had heeded this clear, direct warning from the Bible: "Do not make friends with a hot-tempered man, do not associate with one easily angered."[5] Unequivocally, God's Word instructs us to *leave* the presence of hot-tempered people. If we don't, we—just like Harry—will be burned…and possibly buried under a pile of debilitating debris! Harry died because he *ignored the warning*. Thus, he died needlessly.

The volcanic eruption not only took the life of Harry, it also forever changed Mount St. Helens. It laid waste to itself! The warning bears repeating: Explosive anger cannot be ignored, overlooked, or minimized.

Those who have this kind of explosive temper need to know that their volatility cannot help but damage and sometimes destroy their most meaningful relationships. Their anger bowls are more like basins, with every name and every painful event etched *in molten red*.

The people I call fire eaters—those who swallow their anger—can't keep their anger hidden. Eventually it will flare up in harmful ways. But, people with the opposite problem are what I call flamethrowers —those whose anger flares openly, those who too easily torch and scorch others. Rather than smother their emotions within, they spew their emotions outwardly onto others.

As I've said before, anger, in and of itself, isn't a sin—nor does it necessarily have to lead to sin. But clearly, anger can be the precursor to sin. Uncontrolled anger is *always* wrong and all too often results in offensive words, wrong behavior, even criminal acts.

Flame-throwing anger takes many forms: put-downs and name-calling, profanity and intimidation, property damage and vandalism, personal assaults and murder.

Let's not get the wrong impression, however. Explosive anger isn't necessarily characterized by the screamer shouting insults at strangers, or the mother cruelly mistreating her child for a minor wrongdoing, or the mean neighbor creating noise just to be a nuisance.

Those the Bible describes as hot-tempered can also cause damage in more discreet ways. They might display their anger through constant criticism, behind-the-scenes bullying, intense intimidation, or surreptitious sabotage. Yet regardless of the way a volatile temper is displayed, the Bible doesn't mince words about hotheaded flamethrowers.

Proverbs 14:17 says, "A man of quick temper acts foolishly, and a man of evil devices is hated."[6]

The Four Types of Human Flamethrowers

The first step in dealing with flamethrowers is to recognize the four different types and how their anger is exhibited. Let's take a look at *exploders*, *seethers*, *blamers*, and *abusers*.

1. Exploders: Those prone to sudden eruptive anger

A familiar example of explosive anger and its resulting repercussions is found in Genesis 4:1-16—the biblical account of brothers Cain and Abel. Each man gave an offering to God, each presumably expecting acceptance. As it turned out, one offering was accepted and one wasn't. Abel gave what God wanted to receive. Cain gave what he, himself, wanted to give.

- *The reception?* No surprises here—God received Abel's acceptable offering and rejected Cain's unacceptable one.
- *The reaction?* Cain grew angry and sullen.
- *The remedy?* Simple—God inquired as to the cause of Cain's anger, then told him to do what was right. In doing so, Cain would be accepted.
- *The reality?* If Cain didn't do what was right, sin was waiting to devour him.
- *The result?* Cain invited Abel to go out to the field, where Cain exploded with murderous rage and killed his brother.
- *The repercussion?* Cain left the presence of God, lost his home and livelihood, and lived the remainder of his life as a restless wanderer.

Exploders lash out and behave recklessly. They might normally be reasonable and responsible people, but sometimes their emotions overshadow their thought process and they blow a fuse.

2. Seethers: Those who simmer until their anger boils over

Seethers hold in their anger for long periods—nurturing it with grudges and fantasies of revenge. Their festering emotions also lead to an unforgiving heart toward a past offense or offender. Unforgiveness eventually results in resentment and deep bitterness that harms relationships. When I think of seethers, I recall the words of writer and theologian Frederick Buechner:

> Of the seven deadly sins, anger is possibly the most fun. To lick your wounds, to smack your lips over grievances long past, to roll over your tongue the prospect of bitter confrontations still to come, to savor to the last toothsome morsel both the pain you are given and the pain you are giving back—in many ways it is a feast fit for a king. The chief drawback is that what you are wolfing down is yourself. The skeleton at the feast is you.[7]

When anger is allowed to ferment over a long period of time, it becomes that much more potent. A little bit can do a whole lot of damage. That's why the writer of Hebrews said, "See to it that no one misses the grace of God and that no bitter root grows up to cause trouble and defile many."[8] Seethers are those who have permitted bitterness to take root in their heart, to the detriment of themselves and others. They go through life with a chip on their shoulder and rancor in their spirit, never knowing when their simmering anger is going to boil over.

For these reasons, the Bible instructs us to resolve our conflicts as quickly as possible. Jesus said if you're worshipping at church and remember you have a lingering dispute with someone, you should leave and go take care of it: "Settle matters quickly with your adversary."[9]

How grateful I am for the example my mother set for me in this area. Were it not for her refusal to harbor hurts and rehearse wrongs, my seething anger toward my father might easily have turned me into a resentful, bitter person. My mother kept her anger bowl empty by releasing offenses to God almost immediately upon receiving them.

After totally yielding her life to the Lord, my mother realized how deeply she had been forgiven by the undeserved grace of God. How then could she refuse to forgive others? Over the years, she had realized the danger of holding on to anger, and so she doggedly refused to let it take root in her heart.

3. Blame-shifters: Those who blame others for their faults

In our society, shifting blame to others has been elevated to an art form. People caught speeding tell the traffic cop it is the car's fault for having too much horsepower. Shopaholics blame their massive debt on retailers for displaying irresistible goods. Democrats blame Republicans for America's woes, and Republicans blame Democrats.

We shouldn't be surprised, then, when angry people blame their explosive tendencies on others. Blame-shifters are the exact opposite of self-blamers (those who say, "It's all my fault" to every conflict that arises). In contrast, blamers say, "It's not *my* fault! I'm mad because *you* made me mad. It's *your* fault!"

Have you ever heard the term *blame speak?* Perhaps you've heard these statements come out of someone's mouth—or maybe even your own:

- "I wouldn't have gotten mad if you hadn't made me." *Translation: I'm not responsible for my outbursts—you are.*

- "I can't help it. This is just the way God made me." *Translation: The Creator gave me my temper, so blame Him, not me.*

- "I'm Irish, and we all know the Irish are famous for their fiery temperaments." *Translation: Blame it on my genes.*

- "I didn't mean it." *Translation: I should be let off the hook because my intentions were good, even if my behavior wasn't.*

- "I was just joking. Don't be so uptight." *Translation: You are to blame, not me. You're too sensitive. If you're hurt by my humor, you need to grow thicker skin.*

- "I had lousy role models. Mom and Dad never showed me a better way." *Translation: I shouldn't be held accountable when my parents didn't teach me properly.*

- "Hey, everyone loses their cool now and then." *Translation: I don't take my temper seriously, and neither should you.*

There's an obvious theme running through these statements: I'm not responsible for my actions. Blame-shifting is a strategy used by those who are determined to take their own anger and heap it onto someone else. By refusing to acknowledge their anger, explore where it really comes from, and take responsibility for it, the emotions of blame-shifters stay raw and ready to explode. The apostle John challenged this kind of blame-shifting:

> *"If we claim we have no sin, we are only fooling ourselves and not living in the truth. But if we confess our sins to him, he is faithful and just to forgive us our sins and to cleanse us from all wickedness. If we claim we have not sinned, we are calling God a liar."*[10]

Clearly, God can bring healing and freedom, but we must be willing and courageous enough to face the truth about ourselves and own up to our imperfections. "You will know the truth, and the truth will set you free."[11] The Lord is eager and willing to wash out all the soot that's piled up inside us—but we have to come clean about our anger problem before He can cleanse us.

4. Abusers: Those determined to control others through anger

"He had his hands around my neck, squeezing tighter and tighter," Kayla told me, her voice trembling. "It was the first time I seriously thought, *He's going to kill me. My husband is going to kill me.*"

I had known Kayla for several years and had heard bits and pieces about her background. When I asked her to share her story with me in detail, she was remarkably open. Kayla came from a loving home, but one that always bordered on poverty. Her dad was a hardworking man who didn't make much as a mechanic at the local repair shop.

By the time she was 18, Kayla was ready to leave behind all the financial worries and the constant tension they caused. About that time, a good-looking guy named Mitch appeared, riding not on a white horse, but on a refurbished motorcycle. Still, Kayla convinced herself he might just be the man to whisk her away all the same.

Soon came a starry-eyed romance, promises of a blissful future together, a short dating period, and then an even shorter engagement. Before you knew it, the happy couple was married and living in a run-down duplex, which didn't matter—they were *in love*.

But it wasn't long before this young couple discovered marriage was harder to live out than to dream about. "I do" meant sacrifice, compromise, and hard work. Disillusionment quickly set in. Mitch couldn't hold down a job. When at home, he wasted hours watching television or playing video games. Kayla grew weary of waiting on him hand and foot.

A baby joined the family, then another. Mitch soon lost all interest in playing the role of dutiful, loving father and husband, and his selfish character began to emerge. He also began to drink heavily. He recklessly spent what little money they had and flirted with other women. Then things went from bad to worse.

"Five years into our marriage, Mitch's temper became violent," Kayla recalled. "Our fights had always been heated, but then they got physical. At first, he would get mad and shove me. After a while, he started punching me. On a couple of occasions, I really did think he was going to kill me. These violent episodes became more and more frequent, and went on for several years."

My heart ached as I heard Kayla's sad story. Yet I knew that many good people like Kayla find themselves unexpectedly and undeservedly suffering the consequences of another person's bad temper. We hear sad tales like this, and our indignation prompts us to ask, "Why did you stay? Why didn't you just leave?" I posed those questions to Kayla.

"Looking back now, I know I should've left much sooner," she said. "But it was complicated—not just a matter of picking up and moving on. We eventually had three children, and their safety and protection were my biggest concern. Mitch had become so irrational and unpredictable that I didn't know if he'd try to take the children from me—or hurt them—if I left. I didn't want those beautiful little children to end up in his custody. Not to mention my terror at what he might do to *me*."

There were practical matters as well. Kayla had no real job skills and couldn't have supported the children on her own. Moving in with her parents or other family members—which she did occasionally for short stints—was not a long-term option. She felt trapped.

Of course, Kayla unwittingly contributed to this tragic drama. She realizes now she lacked boundaries and a biblical view of her own self-worth. Her fragile self-esteem prevented her from speaking up or walking out when she should have. Her strong need for security clouded her judgment and justified her decision to stay in a terribly troubled relationship far too long. Still, nothing about her inaction warranted the mistreatment she received.

Fearing for her life, Kayla faced a heartrending decision. Should she leave her husband, or could she stay in the relationship while trying to establish healthy boundaries and ensure her own (and her children's) protection? She prayed, seeking the Lord's guidance. She searched Scripture for direction. She took to heart the Lord's promise in Psalm 32:7-8:

> *"You are my hiding place;*
> *you will protect me from trouble*
> *and surround me with songs of deliverance.*
> *I will instruct you and teach you in the way you should go;*
> *I will counsel you and watch over you."*

Growing Through Ghastly Pain

As Kayla sifted through the rubble of her relationship with Mitch, she learned a number of important lessons. Thankfully, she realized she couldn't manage such difficult transitions on her own—she needed help. She enlisted a mentor, an older woman in her church, who provided sound advice and plenty of encouragement. Together, the two of them developed a plan that, if diligently followed, could give Kayla's marriage a good chance of surviving. They decided Kayla needed to...

Understand the consequences of codependence. If she permitted her husband to continue his disrespectful and damaging behavior, choosing to overlook mistreatment or to acquiesce to his unscriptural demands, she would be contributing to the problem. She memorized a key verse: "A hot-tempered man must pay the penalty; if you rescue him, you will have to do it again" (Proverbs 19:19).

Correct the confusion. Kayla realized that the woman who wants to please God but is not grounded in the Word of God can become captive to an incorrect understanding of biblical submission. All too easily she accepted abuse, thinking it was right even though God says it is wrong. Kayla recognized she needed to study God's Word and seek wise counsel so she could accurately understand the Lord's design for healthy marital relationships.

Build healthy boundaries. This meant clearly communicating acceptable limits of behavior, stating what she would do if her husband crossed the line into inappropriate territory, and following through on her established consequences for boundary violations.

Prepare strategies for safety. Kayla and her mentor knew that abusive cycles do not change overnight. Most often, improvement—if any—is incremental. Therefore, if Kayla were to stay in the marriage, she needed a plan to ensure her physical and emotional safety. She devised a clear-cut strategy for the times when she felt threatened: confide the seriousness of her situation to trustworthy people; be alert to cues that tension was escalating; establish an "escape route" for dangerous situations; and have trusted people on standby to provide help and intervention.

In an ideal world, I could report that these and other strategies transformed Kayla's marriage into a storybook romance. But of course, life is rarely ideal. Despite her efforts, Kayla couldn't piece together the fragile fragments of her broken marriage alone. Without Mitch's cooperation and commitment to change, she was forced to make the painful choice to live apart from Mitch, knowing that to stay would put her own life and the lives of her children in grave danger.

As is so often the case, Mitch didn't let her go easily. He harassed, stalked, and stole from her—employing devious weapons from his anger arsenal. But Kayla's story does have a happy ending. Her Christian friends and caring church community provided resources and shelter when she needed help. A family law attorney at her church offered advice and helped Kayla navigate the legal system. She called upon law enforcement officials to provide protection for herself and her children.

It took several tense and trying years for Kayla to finally feel free of fear. Today she understands her God-given worth and appreciates the respect, care, and love she now receives. Her children, though not without wounds of their own, are thriving in a safe and stable environment. And Kayla is using her hard-won wisdom and insight to help other women find freedom from abuse.

Domestic Violence: A Worldwide Epidemic

We have to wonder how many women and children (and even men) don't experience a happy ending, since sadly the kind of mistreatment Kayla suffered is epidemic:

- Around the world, at least one in every three women has been beaten, coerced into sex, or otherwise abused during her lifetime.[12]

- Nearly one-third of American women (31 percent) report being physically or sexually abused by a husband or boyfriend at some point in their lives.[13]

- In a nationally representative sample of Head Start programs serving low-income children ages three to five, researchers found 17 percent of the children studied had been exposed to domestic violence.[14]

I've heard terror, resignation, helplessness, and hopelessness in the voices of countless callers to *Hope In The Night*—precious people who feel trapped in an emotional prison and alone with nowhere to turn for help, no one to turn to for protection, and no feasible avenue to freedom. "The flamethrowers" had deeply wounded and left no hope for healing.

I've also been privileged to paint the picture for them of a loving, saving God who is able to overcome any obstacle standing in the way of their walking in the freedom Jesus purchased for them. And along with freedom is transformation...becoming the person God created them to be.

I've introduced them to their true Need-Meeter and shared His promises with them. And like Kayla, many have found freedom by trusting God and relying on His strength and guidance. They have experienced healing by finding forgiveness in Christ and extending that forgiveness to their abusers.

> If your genuine desire is to overcome explosive anger, remember: True transformation begins with true repentance.

Outside of Christ, the statistics are grim...and endless. No one would argue that abuse—physical, sexual, spiritual, emotional, or verbal—is a colossal problem in our society and in our world. Whereas exploders are overcome with rage and lash out, abusers have *chronic, ongoing* rage issues. To be sure, both have an anger problem, but abusers take theirs to an entirely new level.

These people are in critical need of intervention and treatment from qualified Christian mental health professionals. Their rage is so far out of control it's unlikely they will learn to contain it without significant intervention, accountability, and help.

Overcoming Explosive Anger

So what to do about all of this out-of-control anger? In Part Three of this book, I will provide numerous practical ways to handle anger by identifying and releasing wounds from the past, preparing ahead of time for anger flare-ups, and managing anger in the heat of the moment. For now, let me give a few ideas to ponder in relation to dealing with an explosive temper (whether your own or someone else's):

Repent. This means agreeing with God that your anger crosses into sinful territory, and then committing to turn away from your wrongdoing. Without rationalizing or excusing your behavior, ask for God's forgiveness and grace. As Paul said, "Godly sorrow brings repentance that leads to salvation and leaves no regret...See what this godly sorrow has produced in you: what earnestness, what eagerness to clear yourselves, what indignation, what alarm, what longing, what concern, what readiness to see justice done."[15] If your genuine desire is to overcome explosive anger, remember: True transformation begins with true repentance.

Recognize your responsibility. It's painful to admit our faults and failings to ourselves and others. But if we're ever going to conquer destructive anger, the process must involve clear-eyed and candid honesty. It must start by telling ourselves, our loved ones, and our Lord the truth. Diminishing the magnitude of the problem or discounting the damage it inflicts will only keep you stuck in unhealthy patterns.

Realize the effects of anger. Unless intense anger is used to confront injustice and correct some wrong, there is nothing good that comes of it. An uncontrolled temper erodes trust in close relationships, creates an atmosphere of fear, thwarts intimacy and communication, and tarnishes your witness and reputation. Until you truly grasp the impact of anger on others—and yourself—you probably won't be motivated to do the work necessary to prevail over the problem.

Request help. Few of us can triumph over significant personal challenges on our own. We need others to provide support, encouragement, and accountability. James tells us, "Confess your sins to each other and pray for each other so that you may be healed."[16] Trying to make changes while going it alone rarely works. God has designed us to draw strength from one another. Success in correcting our deficiencies comes not in isolation, but in the community of fellow sojourners.

Regain trust. When trust is tarnished by the smoky soot of burning anger, this precious treasure can be restored, but it takes some elbow grease—hard work and a determined effort—to reclaim its beautiful luster.

Those you have scorched need to hear you take full responsibility for wrong choices and how your wrong choices are going to become right choices.

- Verbalize that you were totally wrong for reacting in anger.
- Admit your harshness is totally your fault.
- Confess your harshness was selfish and an attempt to control.
- Ask for a willingness to truly forgive you. (This may take time, so do not be demanding.)
- Demonstrate the depth of your remorse by the strength of your resolve to change. (Promises and tears won't build trust, but actions will.) Develop a plan to act differently when you are angry.
- Share your plan, and *be consistent* in carrying it out.

The way to gain trust is to prove you are trustworthy not just when the relationship is easy, but when it is hard—when you feel frustrated, when getting your way has failed. Consistency is the key. Consistently responding without any harshness can, over time, change hearts and restore trust.

> *"Love your [spouses] and do not be harsh with them"*
> (COLOSSIANS 3:19).

※

Unresolved anger is one of the most vexing problems plaguing our society—and the repercussions reverberate across all socioeconomic lines. At this very moment, anger bowls are bursting in homes, in the workplace, at schools, and even in churches. Thankfully, God has not left us to feebly cope on our own. Through the power and the resources He supplies, anger can be managed and used in a healthy way.

Part Two

Detecting
Unquenchable Fires:

Why We Stay Stuck in Unhealthy Anger Patterns

7

Blast from the Past
How Childhood Hurts Kindle Current Anger

> *"Refrain from anger and turn from wrath;*
> *do not fret—it leads only to evil"*
> (PSALM 37:8).

WHEN IT COMES to childhood wounds, it is common to have smoldering embers of which we may not even be aware—remnants we would never suspect could actually spark present-day anger. But when it comes to anger, *out of sight* definitely is not the same as *out of mind*. In fact, hurtful childhood emotions can smolder for decades, be stoked by a current circumstance, and then engulf the unsuspecting in seething rage long after the events that triggered them are forgotten. Let's look at some reasons this happens.

Bonfires from the Beginning

By the time we come of age, most of us have forgotten what a vulnerable state childhood is. At birth we are a bundle of insistent needs and wants, but without the means to meet them on our own. From day one, our dependence on others is absolute. Gradually, we gain both the abilities and the skills we need to fend for ourselves, but our needs are no less real as we grow older. If anything, we become more complex, progressing from foundational needs like food and shelter to the inner needs of significance and security.

Our psychological and spiritual needs are no less vital to our well-being. The truth is we must admit that people need—really *need*—more than just the basics of survival in order to thrive. We need love, significance, and security...and the freedom to be who God created us to be.

If *any* of our needs go unmet, even the intangible ones, we suffer tangible harm. For example, to a child who chronically endures verbal abuse, it doesn't help to say, "Sticks and stones will break my bones, but words will never hurt me." The inner hurt is real and can damage the growth of healthy, trusting relationships. Many of the deepest wounds we receive in life, especially in childhood, are not just a matter of what was done to us, but also what was *withheld* from us.

To a child, such "crimes of omission" can be just as damaging and threatening as overt acts of abuse or oppression. Why? Because in our state of extreme vulnerability before those who have been called by God to care for us, unmet needs can add up to the fear that we might be abandoned altogether. If we grow up carrying these childhood hurts and fears, we can easily become fearful and angry adults.

Incensed for the Innocent

Never will I forget walking toward the exit of a large store and noticing a mother—probably in her late twenties—walking with a shopping cart a few feet in front of me. Toddling along behind her was a cute, curly-haired tyke obviously trying his best to keep up with her. But his little legs were far too short to match her long stride.

Suddenly she whirled around and barked at him in a hateful voice, "If you don't hurry up I'm going to chop your legs off!" With a look of terror, he rushed to get beside the cart.

I was shocked...stunned...I couldn't believe my eyes and ears. Of course, the little fellow's frightened face said it all.

Immediately, I felt angry that any parent would use such an unjustified fear tactic—or in this case, terror tactic—to motivate a child. I picked up my pace and approached her. "Excuse me," I said, intentionally speaking slow and quietly, "I don't know if you realize that children are literalists and what you just said could be terrifying."

I had no idea how the woman would respond, but I couldn't just ignore the verbal abuse. I could no more hold my tongue than she apparently could hold hers.

As we stood there looking at each other, her countenance communicated surprise but also genuine embarrassment. She apparently heard my words and hopefully "got it." To my surprise, she sheepishly took the toddler's hand and, without saying a word, turned and walked off toward the exit.

As I watched them leave, I prayed the Spirit of God would work in the woman's life and fully convict her of the need to permanently change her parenting style. I knew if the mother did not change, that precious little one would carry fear and anger into his adulthood and he might not even be able to pinpoint its source.

It could become what psychologists call "free-floating anger"—disconnected from its cause and purpose. Childhood pain can stoke smoldering embers into a raging blaze in adulthood.

Christian counselor Gary Chapman tells us,

> Whenever we have experienced a series of wrongs over a long period of time, our emotional ability to absorb these wrongs is stretched beyond capacity...We begin to express this anger not toward the people who perpetrated it through past years but toward other people in our present setting. The purpose of our anger is to motivate us to take constructive action with the person who has wronged us, but if we fail to do this, unresolved anger becomes a dark cloud over our lives.[1]

As we attempt to discover why we stay trapped in patterns of anger, it helps to know where the skeletons from our childhood may be hidden. Here are the most common burial grounds:

Emotional Archaeology: Unearthing a Heritage of Heat

Most often, if we retrace the tracks of our unresolved anger back into the past, the trail ends at our parents' doorstep. Who else had such power over our lives? Who more than Mom and Dad shaped our view of God, the world, and our relationship to both? It is often said that parenting isn't for cowards. It's a big job—one that can't be mastered, only practiced. Along the way there are bound to be failures, mistakes, and lapses, even among the most well-intentioned, loving people. That's why, for many of us, the first names ever scrawled across our slips of paper—forming the deepest layer of our anger bowls—read *Mommy, Daddy,* or both.

In fact, many incidents in which a child may feel wounded by parents are inevitable and necessary. A kindergartner might feel abandoned on the first day of school as mother walks away. Yet change and unfamiliar situations are an inescapable part of growing up.

It was our parents who had the ability to either provide or withhold what we needed to survive and thrive. As our immediate role models, it was they who, perhaps unwittingly, taught us how to handle our emotions, especially anger. There is truth in the old adage "With children, more is caught than taught." What we learned spans the spectrum from an inability to express our anger (because our parents wouldn't allow it) to expressing our anger in destructive ways (because our parents would allow it).

Like emotional archaeologists, we must often excavate long-past childhood relationships to answer the question, "Why am I so angry?" The purpose here is not to blame parents for our problems nor bash them for their shortcomings; it's to understand the basis, the foundation, of our emotional makeup so we can identify and correct wrong beliefs we formed about life and how to live it. We need to know and understand *why* we are the way we are so we can have the wisdom to know *how* to change the way we are.

In fact, here's an important thing to remember: Our parents were not—and are not—robots. They were not unpacked fresh from the factory floor the day we were born, made specifically to serve our needs.

They are people, just as vulnerable and just as fallible as anyone. If they are angry themselves, it is surely in response to their own hurts, fears, frustrations, and struggles with injustice.

Chances are, the attitudes and behaviors you have adopted from your parents didn't originate with them. You may be wearing a cloak of unresolved anger that has been passed down in your family for generations.

Knowing this will help you unearth the connections between your past wounds and your present anger without falling into the common trap of pointing fingers and laying blame. The point is not recrimination, but to obtain God's healing.

Finding the Family Fire

Let me tell you about Ryan, a young man who learned in dramatic fashion how to see past his father's angry exterior. Ryan grew up in constant conflict with his father, who he described as a "fuming, withdrawn, cynical alcoholic." Everyone in the family had tried various ways to reach out to him, but they could never get past the wall of his deep pessimism about life and his mistrust of everyone. He kept his wife and children at bay by adopting a menacing, unapproachable posture at home.

Years later, Ryan began to see in himself evidence of his own anger. Girlfriends told him more than once that he was too sarcastic and brooding. His volcanic temper frightened them when all-too-frequent arguments erupted. Ryan quickly recognized his father's imprint on his life, which made him even angrier. He felt helpless to overcome the effects of his upbringing, and he began to blame his past for everything in his life that wasn't going according to plan.

Then one day, he got a rare and healing glimpse into his father's painful past.

"I was riding in the car with my dad, something I hadn't done for years," Ryan told me. "We were listening to news on the radio when a story came on about a local man who had just been arrested for molesting several neighborhood boys. It made me really sad, and I said I couldn't even imagine what those boys must be feeling."

Suddenly, Ryan noticed his father's knuckles were white and his arms were shaking as he struggled to keep a tight grip on the steering wheel. His breathing grew labored and his face turned red. The car hurtled down the highway, faster and faster. Ryan began to fear his father was having a heart attack, which was not far from the truth. Long-buried fear, pain, and anger had swiftly surfaced…and all-consuming rage was now coursing through his body.

"I *know* how it feels," Ryan's father uttered through clenched teeth. "It feels like you want to die, or kill the guy. It's worse than dying. It feels like you'll never be clean again. *Ever.*"

Ryan's father knew all too well what victims of abuse feel because he had been abused as a boy.

Ryan sat in stunned silence, looking at the man he had feared and sometimes even hated, but had never understood until now. His father was no longer just the *perpetrator* of all that angry malice within his family, but also the *victim* of wounds so deep and painful he had stuffed and buried them for 50 years. Ryan experienced compassion for his dad and empathy he'd never felt before, and that became the key to eventually dealing with his own anger. He began reaching into his bowl of anger, releasing to God one tear-stained slip of paper after another…

> God presents Himself in the Bible as the Refiner—the One who refines us so that we come forth as purified silver.

The truth is, we start feeding on conflict, woe, and disappointment long before we grow up to become men and women. Like children playing with matches, we learn early in life what it feels like to get "burned." And though parents are sometimes responsible for childhood hurts and unmet needs, they are by no means the only source.

Children can be wounded by any number of people in any number of ways. Hurt people...*hurt* people.

Some of those wounds can, and do, lead to deep-seated anger later in life. We can feel just as abandoned or mistreated by siblings, peers, teachers—even society at large. Although the severity can vary greatly, it seems virtually impossible for anyone to go through life and not at some point need to release pain into the purifying fire of God. God presents Himself in the Bible as the Refiner—the One who refines us so that we come forth purified.

> *"See, I have refined you, though not as silver;*
> *I have tested you in the furnace of affliction"*
> (Isaiah 48:10).

You Can Transform Your Tomorrows

Without exception, we *all* receive wounds in childhood. We all bear emotional, physical, or spiritual scars. There is no way to turn back the clock and undo what has been done. We must live with the experiences we've been given. But *how* we live with them is entirely up to us. We can nurse our wounds, or ignore them and continue to suffer. Or we can take them to God and be healed by His infinite love and grace. Scripture makes clear which path will lead to healing:

> *"I waited patiently for the Lord; he turned to me and heard my cry.*
> *He lifted me out of the slimy pit, out of the mud and mire;*
> *he set my feet on a rock and gave me a firm place to stand.*
> *He put a new song in my mouth, a hymn of praise to our God.*
> *Many will see and fear and put their trust in the Lord"*
> (Psalm 40:1-3).

※

When we travel back in time to find the source of unresolved anger, the journey will lead to incidents we thought we'd long since forgotten. But undeniably, they still have the power to shape our emotions in the present. No experience, no event, should be dismissed as trivial or childish.

Take each hurt, even the seemingly tiniest, to the Lord and allow Him to apply His healing salve to your soul.

8

Too Hot to Handle

How Being Defensive Heats Up Past Anger

"A hot-tempered person starts fights; a cool-tempered person stops them"
(PROVERBS 15:18 NLT).

IF HUMAN BEINGS were likened to plants, many of them would belong to the hot pepper family.

You know the kind of people I mean: those who defend their every action with a blast of hot, blistering fire, ready to strike at the slightest question. Everything about them says, "Don't get near—or else!" For them, their defensiveness is not just a response to a specific situation; it's a perpetual state of being. Even a simple hello can sound like a stern warning to not cross "the dividing line."

Why is it so easy to get stuck in unhealthy anger patterns? For those who are "pepper people," the answer is clear: Getting caught in habitual, hair-trigger defensiveness is the result of *hanging on to hurts* rather than *handing them over to God*. They nurse their wounds, feed their grudges, and cultivate a victim mentality that walls off their pain from God's healing touch.

Somewhere along the way they were deeply hurt, afraid, frustrated, or offended. Maybe the injury is decades old, dating back to childhood. And maybe something happened just this morning that irritated the wound. In any case, they get angry—a typical response to anything they perceive as threatening.

Processing the "Pepper People" in Our Lives

Just as hot pepper seeds can burn for hours after eating them, a lingering problem develops when pepper people *stay* angry. By refusing to forgive, they remain trapped in a destructive cycle of chronic defensiveness, perpetually poised for "fight or flight."

Several years ago, such a person unexpectedly entered my life. As the newness of the relationship began to wear off, I noticed the quick-to-please behavior also turned into quick-to-anger defensiveness.

After bearing the brunt of several explosions, I became aware of my hypervigilance. Never knowing when an eruption might occur, I began to maintain an almost constant state of expectation. Rather than being able to relax and enjoy an activity together, I was always on high alert.

I felt like a bank guard who stands vigilant, continually looking in all directions for any signs of danger. Never letting your guard down is emotionally draining!

From that experience I gained some insight and some empathy for pepper people. They never allow themselves to completely trust, to completely relax, to completely be themselves. They falsely think that to let go of their pain is to invite even more pain—or worse, to suffer total defeat. They treat everyone as a potential threat. What a lonely and exhausting way to live!

If we have this defensive anger, we set up a firewall around our lives, and we create a forbidding no-man's-land where chronic anger scorches everyone who dares enter. Others quickly get the idea it isn't safe—steer clear!

Who wants a relationship with someone surrounded by emotional barbed wire, guard dogs, and searchlights—someone who "lets 'em have it" first and asks questions later? Is our ironclad defense really worth the price we pay in lost intimacy and love? Most people would answer *no*; yet many of us continue to fall prey to our own disastrous hair-trigger defensiveness.

Diffuse Defensive Anger

If you are trapped in constant defensive anger, chances are you feel you have no choice. It's as if every challenge or insult is a do-or-die fight for survival. All it takes is a harsh tone of voice, a critical comment, getting cut off by another driver, or any one of a thousand other perceived "violations" of your personal rights. Under these conditions, the often-quoted saying "The best defense is a good offense" becomes "The best defense is to decimate your enemies."

That's hardly God's way of looking at things. Jesus said, "In everything, do to others what you would have them do to you, for this sums up the Law and the Prophets."[1] He did not say, "Smash others first before they have a chance to smash you."

If you want to escape the anger snares that are holding you captive, start by assessing your personal state of alertness. Are you ready—at a moment's notice—to demonstrate God's love and forgiveness for others, lay down your "rights," and declare peace? Or are you prone to reach deep into your anger bowl and retrieve a bitter memory, only to vow you'll never forgive *that* incident? The difference between these two responses is what Jesus had in mind when He said:

> *"You have heard that it was said, 'Eye for eye, and tooth for tooth.'*
> *But I tell you, Do not resist an evil person. If someone strikes you on*
> *the right cheek, turn to him the other also. And if someone wants to*
> *sue you and take your tunic, let him have your cloak as well.*
> *If someone forces you to go one mile, go with him two miles"*
> (Matthew 5:38-41).

Here's the point: Being excessively defensive is as hazardous as building your house in a minefield. If the constant stress doesn't get you, sooner or later an explosion will. And chances are, your explosions will do just as great harm to those nearest and dearest to you.

As Proverbs 29:22 reminds us, "An angry man stirs up dissension, and a hot-tempered one commits many sins."

There's no way around it: Defensiveness—focusing only on what we want to *protect*—just compounds whatever painful and possibly legitimate reason we had for being angry. Becoming defensive makes matters far worse by searing our relationships and blocking our ability to grow through adversity. And the longer we don't allow God to pry our fingers off of our anger bowls, the less opportunity there will be for Him to use our hands for good, to reach out and help those in need.

> The longer we don't allow God to pry our fingers off our anger bowls, the less opportunity there will be for Him to use our hands for good.

Something's Got to Give

When Jimmy called me on *Hope In The Night*, he reluctantly—and almost apologetically—described himself as shell-shocked in his marriage to Diana. He explained that, by most measurements, he had little to complain about in the relationship. Diana was a brilliant and successful professor at a prominent university. She was a good mom and a reliable partner in family affairs. After ten years of marriage, Jimmy and Diana were still deeply attracted to each other and often joked about having had the world's longest honeymoon.

"So what's the problem?" I asked Jimmy.

"Maybe I am just an overly demanding person, but I honestly don't think so," he said. "Diana has always been sensitive to criticism, but lately it has come to the point where she reacts like she is under full-scale attack over the smallest things. She raises the drawbridge and goes into siege mode. Then there's no way to go near her without getting an arrow through my chest."

Jimmy's vivid choice of words is a perfect description of life with a defensively angry person. In response to any perceived threat, the person withdraws behind formidable fortifications erected around his or her heart—and then fires flaming arrows at anyone within range. Diana's angry defensiveness had simply become "too hot to handle."

"It's like she's got to prove to the whole world that she is smarter, stronger, and better than everyone else," Jimmy said sadly. "It breaks my heart to think about what may have caused her to feel so insecure in who she really is. But it's also sapping the life out of our relationship. Now *I* am starting to feel like I'm on the defensive all the time. Something's got to give."

Jimmy rightly recognized Diana's struggle with defensive anger as the result of some past wound that caused her to feel afraid and insecure. When people are angry, there is a reason. Jimmy also came to realize he was more than just an occasional bystander—he had become a regular target of Diana's unresolved anger, or the bull's-eye, if you will.

The truth is, defensively angry people are often hardest on those who love them the most. Their dearest relationships frequently come under intense stress and strain. Why? Let's take a look.

The Downsides of Defensive Anger

1. Defensiveness Stifles Communication

It is hard work to talk through the many thorny issues arising in the normal course of any intimate relationship, even when both people are open and willing to listen. A delicate balance of give and take, advance and retreat is required. But when one or both consider any "give" to be tantamount to treason, conversation can quickly turn combative and vital compromise grows vastly more difficult.

Chances are, someone will have to surrender unconditionally before peace can return to the household. And guess which person usually waves the white flag? Not the doggedly defensive one. Over time our family and friends grow tired of constant capitulation and simply stop talking to us about sensitive matters. This much is certain: When communication starts to break down, divisions develop and relationships are in trouble.

The antidote for defensive division is letting God's healing love bring reconciliation, and then passing that love on to others. The Bible sums up love's restorative power:

"Love is patient, love is kind. It does not envy,
it does not boast, it is not proud. It is not rude, it is not self-seeking,
it is not easily angered, it keeps no record of wrongs.
Love does not delight in evil but rejoices with the truth.
It always protects, always trusts, always hopes, always perseveres"
(1 CORINTHIANS 13:4-7).

When we give up defensiveness as a way of relating to others, communication flows more freely and loving relationships grow stronger and healthier.

2. Defensiveness Preempts Accountability

Here is an unavoidable truth: No one is perfect. Each of us is a work in progress, with room to grow and much to learn. Every day is a new opportunity to gain maturity and wisdom. For that reason, the world is our classroom, and our relationships are among our most valuable teachers. They serve as mirrors in which we can see ourselves more clearly. In countless ways, those closest to us help hold us accountable for our words and actions.

The problem with our defensiveness is that it throws a monkey wrench into the process. We dodge responsibility, missing out on the opportunity to learn from our mistakes. The clamor of combat may drown out the people who we think could possibly hurt us, but it also prevents us from hearing God's gentle corrections through those He would use to help change us.

Solomon wrote, "He who listens to a life-giving rebuke will be at home among the wise. He who ignores discipline despises himself, but whoever heeds correction gains understanding" (Proverbs 15:31-32). That's great counsel for anyone who uses defensive anger to keep accountability at bay.

3. Defensiveness Makes a Mountain Out of Every Last Molehill

Over the years, I have learned to trust the deep wisdom in this simple phrase: *Choose your battles carefully.* This is never more true than when I am angry. To follow this advice, I try to stop before acting on my anger and ask myself:

—Am I in the right?

—What benefit will come from fighting this battle?

—Even if I succeed, will it do more harm than good?

—How would Jesus respond to this situation?

Believe me, I don't always get it right. But more than once I've avoided making a costly mistake by counting the cost before initiating a confrontation. As Jesus said, "Suppose a king is about to go to war against another king. Will he not first sit down and consider whether he is able with ten thousand men to oppose the one coming against him with twenty thousand?" (Luke 14:31).

It's just common sense, really. Yet when you are ensnared in endless cycles of defensive anger this kind of strategic thinking is next to impossible. When every offense, no matter how small, feels like a matter of life and death, it is unthinkable to simply let it go. When you haven't surrendered your past pain to God, you may feel compelled to react to every new threat with fresh anger whether it makes sense or not. Unable to really afford another fight, you are equally convinced you can't afford to pass one up.

A king like *that*, I'm sure Jesus would say, is doomed to defeat—or at least to poverty from constant warfare. The only solution is not confrontation but rather submission—submitting our anger wounds to God's healing touch. Then we can seek the wisdom of God, surrender all our battles to Him, and trust Him to bring peace and reconciliation.

4. Defensiveness Keeps You from Dealing with the Cause of Anger

After our conversation, Jimmy told Diana he was tired of living in a war zone. He invited her to participate in "peace talks" with him and have a counselor on *Hope In The Night* mediate. It wasn't easy for her to see past the feeling that she was once again under attack, but she eventually agreed.

Months later, I spoke with Diana about the experience. She said, "The breakthrough came when I realized being defensive and fighting with Jimmy over every little thing was preventing me from seeing the truth: He wasn't the source of my anger at all. It was like being so focused on the smoke, that I had no idea where the fire was."

As it turned out, her hidden fire had been burning for a long time. Growing up with three highly competitive older brothers, Diana came to believe she had to work ten times harder than most people just to be considered "good enough." By the time she went to college, she was already on high alert. But it was there her habit of expressing razor-sharp defensive anger really took hold. As a young graduate student in a field dominated by men, she felt she had been "dropped behind enemy lines." Unfortunately, her advisors all seemed to be cut from the same chauvinistic cloth, and their critique of her work was often belittling, sarcastic, and overly personal.

"I decided no one would ever treat me that way again," Diana told me. "The sad thing is I turned into the very sort of angry person I was trying to protect myself from."

By being overly defensive and building impregnable walls, Diana had prevented herself from getting to the bottom of why she was mad in the first place. Eventually, hardly a day went by when she didn't find some petty reason to project all her pain and anger onto Jimmy. It was unfair to him and kept her stuck in a self-reinforcing cycle of unresolved anger. Thankfully, she finally broke through it.

※

Civil rights leader Martin Luther King Jr. once said, "Darkness cannot drive out darkness; only light can do that. Hate cannot drive out hate; only love can do that."[2]

A life of angry defensiveness cannot drive out pain and fear. Only God's healing grace can do that when we surrender ourselves into His care.

Fire and Ice

How a Controlling Spirit Fuels Chronic Anger

"A gentle answer turns away wrath, but a harsh word stirs up anger"
(PROVERBS 15:1).

BECAUSE OF OUR unprecedented access to technology, to some degree we all have control issues—so much so that we are not fully aware of their influence on how we think and the role they play in our problems with runaway anger.

At the touch of a button or the flick of a switch, we exercise a level of command over our environment that our ancestors would never have imagined possible. We have thermostats to regulate room temperature, lightbulbs to "extend" the day, timers on everything from coffeepots to automatic sprinkler systems, and cars and planes that can condense months of travel by foot into a few hours' journey.

Kids and adults alike play home video games and watch what happens in the world using a device called a "controller." We *order* our food, *manage* our careers, *master* our money, and *secure* our retirement. The list could go on and on. Clearly, we've made control a way of life.

The Cop Who Copped an Attitude

One Christmas holiday years ago when I was a youth director, a family in the church I served invited me and two friends to their vacation home in Crested Butte, Colorado—they wanted to teach us how to ski! What a perfect place to spend time with friends and celebrate the season…or so I thought.

On Christmas evening, with great excitement, Sandy, Barbara, and I packed my car and headed out from Dallas, taking turns driving the long stretches of open road. About three-fourths of the way into our trip, I was behind the wheel when we were coming down mountainous Raton Pass into Colorado. I looked in the rearview mirror and saw what sparks apprehension in most of us—the flashing lights of a patrol car.

"Oh, no!" I nearly shouted. "I can't believe it!" Barbara and Sandy looked back and saw the pulsating bursts of the police lights. In unison, they let out a groan.

Immediately I looked at the speedometer. I breathed a huge sigh of relief when I saw I wasn't exceeding the speed limit. (I've been known to say, "I don't drive fast; I just fly low." Fortunately that morning, I wasn't flying!)

"I know I wasn't speeding," I said confidently and guilt-free as I pulled onto the shoulder of the highway. After the police car came to a stop behind me, I opened the driver's side door and hopped out.

"Lady, get back in that car!" the officer barked. He punctuated his command with a pointed finger stabbing the air in my direction. "Now!"

Feeling scolded, I retreated back into my car. The officer sat in his car for a long time, doing who knows what, while the three of us waited in silence. Finally, he swaggered up to the car in his uniform—knee-high boots, pants flaring at the thighs like British hunting breeches, and the kind of hat forest rangers wear.

He leaned over to survey the car's occupants, then growled, "License and registration." After handing him the papers, he looked at them and said matter-of-factly, "I'm going to ticket you for speeding."

Though surprised, I tried to sound cooperative. "Sir, I'm sure I wasn't speeding."

For several long seconds, he just glared at me as if I'd said the stupidest thing he'd ever heard. Finally, in a tone dripping with condescension, he said, "Lady, with these hazardous road conditions, you should have dropped your speed by ten miles-per-hour. That's the law."

"Officer, I'm sorry. I've never heard of this law."

He had his quick retort in place. "Ignorance of the law is no excuse! You were driving recklessly, endangering yourself and others. I'm going to issue you a citation. Don't blame me—blame yourself."

I was incensed. *A ticket for not slowing down, even though I was going the speed limit? That's ridiculous!* But I still tried to explain, "Well sir, in Texas…"

Mid-sentence, he turned on the heels of his shiny boots and strutted back toward his car. Immediately I felt my cheeks get hot, my heart start pounding, and my blood pressure soar.

Let me point out that I have tremendous respect for law enforcement officers, but this particular one had a bad attitude to match his big ego. "I think he needs to read *How to Win Friends and Influence People*," I muttered sarcastically.

Then things got worse.

Returning to our car, he demanded, "Follow me back into town. You have to pay your fine now."

"But…can't I just send a check in later?"

"No," he insisted. "Follow me—*now*."

My "Go Directly to Jail" Card

I couldn't believe it! We had no choice but to drive about 15 minutes to the police station. Upon arrival, the officer didn't say a word. He just pointed with obvious disdain. I felt like I had just drawn the orange "Go Directly to Jail" card in the game of Monopoly.

With a hard stride, I marched in, paid the fine, and marched out. I opened the car door—with unusual strength—and uncharacteristically slammed the door shut. Barbara and Sandy fell silent.

During the entire time of our detour, my teeth were clenched and beads of perspiration formed on my forehead even though the temperature outside was an icy 20 degrees Fahrenheit. When we finally resumed our northward trek, I noticed my knuckles were white from clutching the steering wheel so tightly.

> Discerning our own anger cues can help us avoid trouble.

What I learned (besides the need to reduce my speed in snowy conditions if I don't want a ticket!) was just how much my angry feelings impacted me physically. For a person who thought she didn't have any anger issues, I exhibited *all* the symptoms of someone who had them! (Well, almost.)

What Are "Anger Cues"?

At those times when we really are angry but won't admit it, everyone else around us knows it! That's because we give off "anger cues." Our anger may be *internal*, but its expression is *external*.

Anger and volcanoes have similar qualities. Before an eruption, there's a gurgling beneath the surface, a swirling series of events that creates pressure. In fact, scientists know to look for cues that a volcano is about to erupt, including the release of steam and gases, small earthquakes and tremors, and the swelling of a volcano's slopes.

Similarly, the human body has physical reactions when it experiences anger. These anger cues alert us that we are experiencing a potentially explosive emotion.

Discerning our own anger cues can help us avoid trouble. Likewise, being aware of the signs of anger in others can alert us to avoid an angry response or protect ourselves by "donning fire-retardant clothing." A biblical example of an anger cue is Jonathan's loss of appetite stemming from his father's unjust, shameful treatment of his close friend, David: "Jonathan got up from the table in fierce anger...he did not eat, because he was grieved at his father's shameful treatment of David."[1]

We may not all express anger the same way, but once we have identified our anger cues, we will be in a better position to deal with this emotion in ourselves as well as in others. Then we can take the steps necessary to avoid an explosion of anger.

Anger Cues

- churning stomach
- clenched fists
- clenched teeth
- decreased appetite
- dry mouth
- rapid breathing
- rapid walking
- flushed face
- harsh/coarse/sarcastic language
- increased perspiration
- loud sighing/groaning
- racing heart
- rapid/high-pitched speech
- shutting down verbally
- tearful eyes
- tense muscles
- twitches/anxious behaviors (such as tapping a pencil, shaking a foot)
- becoming unusually hot or cold

On the flip side of control issues, there is nothing wrong with a desire for order and structure in our lives. For example, I'm grateful for refrigeration that preserves food and systems of hygiene that control disease.

Letting go of control doesn't mean we have to take a debilitating step back into the Dark Ages. But with such immense power at our disposal, it's easy to see how we learn to take for granted our ability to master just about every aspect of our lives. When control is curtailed, it can be *catastrophic*—for those who struggle with anger and for those all around them. Control, it turns out, is a dangerously addictive commodity.

The Bible says,

> *"What causes fights and quarrels among you? Don't they come from your desires that battle within you? You want something but don't get it. You kill and covet, but you cannot have what you want. You quarrel and fight. You do not have, because you do not ask God. When you ask, you do not receive, because you ask with wrong*

motives, that you may spend what you get on your pleasures...
But he gives us more grace. That is why Scripture says:
'God opposes the proud but gives grace to the humble'"
(JAMES 4:1-3,6).

When problems break out like scattered brush fires in our lives, trying to contain and control them on our own only leaves us ultimately sitting in an ash heap, smoldering in angry frustration.

The Truth About Control

If we really want to find freedom from destructive anger, a good place to start is relinquishing control of anything and everything around us. Here are a few points to remember about control:

Control is impossible. It is an inescapable truth that everything in God's creation is in a state of constant motion. Nothing remains the same. Even in the depth of frozen winter, spring is already present in seeds beneath the ground. As the tide flows out to sea, it's already gathering itself to return.

The tallest mountains experience erosion, and all that remains of many great civilizations of the past are a few stones stacked together. Indeed, life is like a flowing river that sometimes thunders in flash-floods and other times meanders lazily through broad meadows—but it never stops changing the landscape.

Some people are called "control freaks." They try to control everything and everyone. However, attempting to control circumstances and people—to step into that continual current and command it to turn right or turn left or be still—is ultimately futile. It simply cannot be done. When we approach life as the absolute masters of our fate and controllers of our destiny, we are doomed already to failure, frustration, and anger.

It doesn't have to be that way. We can admit we've been mistaken and have invested ourselves in an impossible task.

It's time to let God heal us of this need to be overly controlling along with the anger that comes with it when we don't get our way.

We must surrender our wishes and wants, our desires and demands to the sovereignty of our loving and compassionate God.

Control is a heavy and unnecessary burden. In the Bible, we see an example of one sister's attempt to exert control over her sibling. Martha was angry with her sister, Mary. Jesus had come to stay at their house, so there was work to do and food to prepare.

The Bible says Martha was "distracted with much serving," and she perceived Mary as no help at all. She felt abandoned to do the heavy lifting while Mary sat listening to Jesus speak.

Finally, Martha had had enough. It was time to force Mary into the kitchen. She approached Jesus and said, "Lord, don't you care that my sister has left me to do the work by myself? Tell her to help me!"[2]

Oh, how my heart goes out to Martha. How many times have I tried to enlist God in my efforts to control something I didn't like? I can feel the familiar weight of responsibility on her shoulders, can't you? Her face was probably flush from frustration as her voice rang with indignation.

Jesus responded to her put-upon attitude this way: "Martha, Martha...you are worried and upset about many things, but only one thing is needed. Mary has chosen what is better, and it will not be taken away from her."[3]

Some might hear stinging censure in Jesus' words, but I interpret them as a compassionate invitation for Martha to lay down her needless burden of worry and control. I can imagine Him saying, "There is a better way. Mary has chosen it, and so can you." That way is called trust, putting God first and allowing Him to guide your life. Martha needed to make an important trip back to the kitchen to empty her anger bowl, place it at the back of a cabinet, and leave it there for good.

Control is God's business, and not having this heavy responsibility is His gift to us. Assuming the right to control our lives according to our own will is dangerous arrogance—and sinful pride. Job learned the same lesson. When he assumed too much, God replied,

"Who is this that darkens my counsel with words without knowledge?

Brace yourself like a man; I will question you, and you shall answer me.
Where were you when I laid the earth's foundation? Tell me, if you
understand. Who marked off its dimensions? Surely you know!
Who stretched a measuring line across it?"
(Job 38:2-5).

It was a well-deserved rebuke. But like an earthly father who refuses to give a little child the keys to the family car, God's authority and sovereignty are intended for our protection and well-being.

> God wants you to seek His answer for anger quickly before it singes your heart and burns the bridges of your relationships.

No, it is not possible for us to control every facet of life. But the good news is that the Creator of the whole universe has promised to do it for us.

Jesus said, "Do not worry about your life, what you will eat or drink; or about your body, what you will wear. Is not life more important than food, and the body more important than clothes?"[4] You can't control it anyway, according to Jesus, so trust your Father to provide.

Jesus also said, "Who of you by worrying can add a single hour to his life?"[5] Let go, and release the stress and tension that accompanies the need to control.

Furthermore, Jesus said, "Come to me, all you who are weary and burdened, and I will give you rest. Take my yoke upon you and learn from me, for I am gentle and humble in heart, and you will find rest for your souls. For my yoke is easy and my burden is light."[6]

There is nothing light about the burden of control. Give it to God, and end your angry turmoil.

What Is the Quick Answer to Anger?

Few people know the importance of a quick answer more than the members of a First Response TEAM (Tactical Emergency Asset Management). When disaster strikes, they rapidly deploy communications technologies to the scene, ensuring that voice, video, and data capabilities are fully functional among the attending agencies.

When you sense a disastrous surge of anger, it's just as vital that you too learn to respond quickly. If not, your anger could prove catastrophic.

The possibility of anger remains ever present. A spark of irritation can be ignited intentionally by hurtful people or even unintentionally by those who love you. God wants you to seek His answer for anger quickly before it singes your heart and consumes your relationships. "A gentle answer turns away wrath, but a harsh word stirs up anger."[7]

Many people try to make the solution for anger more complex than it should be. Of course, there will always be multiple approaches and steps to managing anger (and I will cover many of them later in this book). However, at the risk of sounding too simplistic, I will present here what for decades I have called...

The Quick Answer to Anger

If I boiled down managing anger to the most basic precepts, I believe you could provide a viable solution with two steps.

Step 1: Ask—Can I change this situation?
Step 2: Action—If you *can, change* it. If you *can't, release* it.

Let's start with the first step: Can you change what angers you? Answer *yes* or *no*—that's it.

Now consider the second step: If you answered *yes*, you are angry about something you *can* change—so change it.

- If the door squeaks, oil it.
- If the faucet leaks, fix it.

If you answered *no*, you are angry about something you *cannot* change—so release it.

- If your house burns down, release it.

- If your loved one dies, release that person.

If your house does burn down, only by emotionally releasing the pain of your loss can you rebuild your life, and possibly your home. Being angry about a burned house or a buried loved one—or anyone who caused either—will not change the situation; it will only make matters worse.

But How Do I Surrender?

Here's the point: God has provided an antidote to poisonous anger that comes from trying to be in control all of the time. All it costs us is *surrender to His will*.

More than 300 years ago, a French priest named Jean-Pierre de Caussade put it this way:

> "[True surrender to God is] a state in which one discovers how to belong wholly to God through the complete and total assignment of all rights over oneself—over one's speech, actions, thoughts and bearing; the employment of one's time and everything related to it. There remains one single duty. It is to keep one's gaze fixed on the master one has chosen and to be constantly listening so as to understand and hear and immediately obey his will."[8]

Yes, we are conditioned by culture and coaxed by human nature to believe we can achieve control over our lives. And yes, it makes us angry when our efforts to keep things and people in line don't work as we intended.

The more energy we pour into the impossible task of control, the more we place ourselves at the mercy of runaway rage. Let go. Release control. Allow God to reign over every aspect of your life, and soon you'll find joy in seeing *calm* rather than *control* characterize your life.

Self-Inflicted Flames

How Guilt and Shame Ignite Harmful Anger

"Be quick to listen, slow to speak, and slow to get angry. Human anger
does not produce the righteousness God desires"
(James 1:19-20 nlt).

Do you know someone who struggles with any of these burning
questions?

> Why do I feel so angry at times?
>
> Why do I lash out at others over little things?
>
> What can I do before my anger does lasting damage?

If the "someone" happens to be you, consider this: In the best-case
scenario, finding an answer is a simple matter of analyzing cause and
effect. You retrace your steps back to the spark that ignited your anger,
the cause, then you set about addressing the consequences, the effect.

But the problem is the "cause" isn't always obvious. This chapter
is devoted to exploring one possibility especially easy to overlook. It
goes like this:

If your anger has ever erupted in disproportionate hostility toward
another person, it may be the intended victim was really *yourself.*

Typically, anger toward yourself comes from personal failure, disappointment, or being taken advantage of—all with painful consequences.
These include living in a way that's far from God's ideal and your own.

Whatever the cause, anger at yourself can easily detonate like a bomb and damage those around you.

Collateral Damage

When I met Lily, she was on top of the world. A vivacious woman in her late twenties, she was hired as a full-time member of the youth ministry team at a growing, dynamic church.

She talked a mile a minute about her new position, bursting with ideas and energy. It was obvious she cared deeply about young people and the problems they face in our permissive culture.

Neither of us could have guessed, when we spoke again a few months later, that she would have fallen from the top of the world to the bottom of the barrel.

"I quit my job," she told me abruptly, fighting back tears. Her spirited enthusiasm was gone, replaced by a defeated demeanor. "I let everyone down, and I haven't got a clue how to fix it."

Lily's pain was palpable, and my heart went out to her.

She took a deep breath and plunged into her story.

"I have a lot of anger inside that gets out of control sometimes," she confessed. "I've always thought people who criticized my temper were just too touchy and thin-skinned. But I can't run from it anymore. Now I *know* I have a problem."

Not long after she started working at the church, a troubling pattern began to emerge in Lily's relationship with some of the young people. She took a few especially troubled ones under her wing and made it her mission to guide and disciple them. Perhaps because of this investment, she began to take it personally anytime they broke the youth group's rules. Naturally, it was part of her job to be sure the teens adhered to expected standards while at church.

The problem lay in how angry she became when one of "her kids" failed to live up to those expectations. On several occasions, she publicly yelled at them in a rage.

"I convinced myself tough love was the way to get through to them...

to save them from themselves," Lily said. "I thought I was doing them a favor in the long run."

She was forced to change her mind after a traumatic incident during the youth group's weeklong summer camp. One night, after lights out, she caught three girls drinking from a whiskey bottle one of them had smuggled from home in a suitcase.

"When I think about that night, I can't explain why I got so mad," Lily admitted. "Something inside me just snapped."

Enraged, Lily berated the girls. And then the unthinkable happened. She grabbed the bottle of alcohol and hurled it against the wall. A shard of glass rebounded and struck her in the head, leaving a gash on her scalp that bled profusely.

The terrified teenagers ran for help, and soon the entire cabin, counselors, and staff came to see what happened.

"I thank God I was the one who got hurt and not one of them," she said. "I feel like some kind of monster. I know I looked like one, too, standing there with blood pouring down my face.

"Even though they shouldn't have been drinking, my reaction was over the top. How could I get so angry with them?"

"Perhaps they weren't the reason for your anger at all," I suggested. "Maybe they were only standing in for the *real* target of your disappointment and outrage."

"What target?" she asked skeptically.

"Well, is there something in the kids' behavior that reminds you of someone else? Yourself, perhaps?" I was only probing, but apparently I had struck a nerve.

Lily began to cry in earnest. When she regained her composure enough to speak, the rest of the story emerged.

On her eighteenth birthday, Lily's friends threw her a party when she was supposed to be at soccer practice. Their "gift" to her was a six-pack of beer and a few bottles of tequila pilfered from parents' liquor cabinets. By dinnertime, Lily was in a drunken stupor and she staggered home.

When she stumbled through the front door of her house, everything was quiet. It appeared no one was home. She felt immediate relief to be able to sneak upstairs to her room unnoticed. Until—

"Surprise! Happy birthday!"

"Suddenly, the house was full of happy, laughing people all looking at me," Lily recalled. "My grandparents and aunts and uncles were there. Church people. My *pastor*.

"I'll never forget the look on my mother's face when she realized the state I was in. I reeked of booze, my eyes were bloodshot, and every word that came out of my mouth was slurred.

"I blurted out a terrible obscenity and tried to run up the stairs, but had to be carried instead. There was nowhere left to hide after that." Thankfully, the humiliation that night became a turning point in Lily's life—evidence of God's capacity to transform any defeat into victory.

Lily abandoned the rebellious, self-destructive path she had started down and devoted herself instead to a life of service to God. Her family forgave her and helped her form new values and habits.

There was just one problem. Through it all, Lily never forgave *herself.* Years later, her anger still burned at her unwise choices and actions. And her anger was hot enough to scorch anyone who got in its path.

The misbehaving teenagers in Lily's youth group became unwitting "mirrors" who had reflected Lily's own troubled past and fanned the flames of her longtime anger at herself.

Arson Investigation 101

Here's the lesson in Lily's story: Unresolved rage directed at yourself is like a pressure cooker without a relief valve—as the underlying source grows hotter, pent-up force continues to build until it explodes.

Even after the explosion, superhot anger spills into chronic depression, self-sabotage, broken relationships, or inexplicable outbursts toward others.

When these things happen, there are two questions you need to ask that will lead to help and healing: Why am I so mad at myself? And, why can't I forgive myself? Here are four flammable possibilities:

1. Good-Guilt Gary and Shame-Filled Shannon

Justifiable guilt is a *good* thing. Yes, that's right—there is such a thing as "good guilt." It is that shrill alarm that blares in your conscience and warns that you've strayed off course.

In fact, admitting you are guilty of sin and in need of God's forgiveness is the first step you must take to receive the salvation He offers through faith in Christ.

Think about it: No one seeks a pardon for a crime he doesn't believe he committed. In order to be free of guilt before God, you must first take full responsibility for what you did wrong. As the apostle John wrote: "If we claim to be without sin, we deceive ourselves and the truth is not in us" (1 John 1:8).

What happens when you get stuck somewhere between confessing your sins and receiving the freedom of God's forgiveness?

That's what happens to Shame-Filled Shannon. What if she can't take the next step and let go of her guilt, leaving it in God's hands, where it belongs? The answer is that her healthy guilt will become distorted into something God never intended His children to feel: shame.

The difference between Good-Guilt Gary and Shame-Filled Shannon is enormous. Consider these contrasting statements:

Gary:	"I know what I did was wrong."
Shannon:	"I am a terrible person because of what I did."
Gary:	"I ask God to forgive me and show me how I can make amends."
Shannon:	"No amount of punishment can repay what I owe."
Gary:	"I have a lot to learn from my mistakes."
Shannon:	"If I were a good person, my mistakes would never have happened in the first place."

You can easily see that proper feelings of guilt open the door for repentance, restoration, and right living.

Shame, on the other hand, leads only to more shame—with no way out—and leaves you with a lifetime of self-loathing.

Eventually shame makes you angry at yourself for failing so miserably and you feel unworthy of God's love. In fact, shame and anger go hand in hand, beginning in earliest childhood.

Shame generates a cycle of anger, whether we receive it from someone else—a teacher, parent, spouse, or boss—or mercilessly heap it on ourselves. Most important of all, anger you direct inward rarely stays there—it eventually surges to the surface.

Lily learned these things the hard way. In letting her guilt turn to shame, she lit the fuse on a volatile bomb of anger aimed at herself but it inadvertently landed on innocent bystanders.

The apostle John said, "If we confess our sins, he is faithful and just and will forgive us our sins and purify us from all unrighteousness."[1] If shame is the source of your anger, own up to your guilt, agree with God that you are forgiven, and then...let it go!

2. Perfectionist Patty

Someone once remarked, "Perfectionists are the only people on earth who fail 100 percent of the time." At first glance, this statement seems absurd. After all, no group of people works harder at success than perfectionists. They take pride in their high standards and never rest in the quest for excellence.

Failure? Not an option for the perfectionist.

But look again, and you'll see a tragic truth in the statement. By definition, perfectionism is a pattern of thinking that demands all areas of life be flawless. Anything less than perfect is unacceptable.

Take Perfectionist Patty, who *never* accomplishes precisely what she sets out to do. Why? Because flawless perfection in this world is simply unattainable. It can't be had at any price. Her achievements may be excellent or optimal—but they are never always *perfect*. Therefore, she can't help but feel like a failure.

If Perfectionist Patty fails to understand the pitfalls of perfectionism, she is doomed to spend her life running ever harder and faster to win a prize that doesn't exist. No matter what she achieves, it will never be good enough.

And *that* is a ticking time bomb—one on the verge of detonating from unavoidable repeated defeat.

Of course, if you are a demanding perfectionist, who are you most likely to blame for your constant frustration and failure? That's right—yourself! You'll conclude you simply *are* a failure, and you imagine God judging you as harshly as you judge yourself. And then you become consumed by your own self-diagnosed insufficiency.

But let's be clear: God doesn't share our illusions of human perfection. He knows better than anyone that His children are a work in progress and always will be. As Isaiah 40:6-8 tells us:

> *"All men are like grass,*
> *and all their glory is like the flowers of the field.*
> *The grass withers and the flowers fall,*
> *because the breath of the LORD blows on them.*
> *Surely the people are grass.*
> *The grass withers and the flowers fall,*
> *but the word of our God stands forever."*

Oliver Wendell Holmes Jr., once said, "The secret of my success is that at an early age I discovered I was not God."[2]

3. Condemnation Carl

Perhaps you live at the opposite end of the spectrum, among people who need no evidence that they'll never be perfect. Maybe you are painfully aware of your seemingly innumerable flaws because barely a minute goes by when you aren't reminded of them by a relentless critic—your own thoughts. It is as if a two-bit judge has set up court in your mind, banging the gavel all day long and handing out harsh verdicts left and right.

- Lost your car keys? *Bang! You haven't got the brains of a turnip!*

- Burned the lasagna? *Bang! You are a sorry excuse for a cook!*
- Ate a donut in the break room at work? *Bang! You are a glutton!*
- Had a lustful thought? *Bang! You're a lukewarm hypocrite!*
- Tripped over the rug? *Bang! You're a klutz!*

The point is, we take a lot of abuse from inside our own heads—perhaps far more than we would if someone were following us around shouting insults.

And if you grew up with a critical parent, it may be especially difficult for you to tune out the voice of condemnation in your conscience.

This daily torrent of negativity can lead to self-blame, self-loathing, and self-combustion. Such all-consuming anger can't help but singe and scorch those nearby.

> Anytime the voice of condemnation in your conscience berates you, answer it with scriptures describing God's view of you.

Freedom lies in asking yourself, *Is this the way God sees me? Are these labels He would attach to me: loser, moron, failure, rotten, hopeless?* The answer is obvious: Never! God's thoughts toward His children are rooted in His unfathomable love. The proof is in His sacrifice for your sake. This is how the Bible describes His love for you:

> *"This is how we know what love is: Jesus Christ laid down his life for us...This then is how we know that we belong to the truth, and how we set our hearts at rest in his presence whenever our hearts condemn us. For God is greater than our hearts, and he knows everything"*
> (1 JOHN 3:16,19-20).

Anytime the voice of condemnation in your conscience berates you, answer it with scriptures describing God's view of you. In the light of

His Word, hateful "self-inflicted flames" will dissipate and a strong sense of self-worth will emerge. Let God's exclamations of love drown out those whispers of accusation and condemnation.

The Importance of Seeing Yourself Through God's Eyes

A few days after *Hope For The Heart* began airing on March 3, 1986, I received a letter—which I still have to this day. I've kept it because it's the voice of countless others who struggle with low self-esteem and have no idea of their value to the One who created them and died for them.

The letter was from a former high school beauty queen who grew up with a father who repeatedly told her, "You'll never amount to anything. You're nothing!" And a boyfriend who berated, "You dingbat... you miserable slut!" I remember hurting for her as I read the letter.

She was writing to say she felt like she had little value. Although she had become a Christian, the tapes from the past kept replaying in her mind.

In the providence of God, she married a man who was, in her own words, "a wonderful, fruit-bearing Christian." Then she wrote, "But he has the same problem." Ending her letter, she asked, "Could you help us?"

My first thought was, *I wish I could have a month with her, going over what it means to have her identity in Christ.* But that wasn't possible, so I immediately drafted a response reassuring her of Christ's presence in her life, of her being a new creation in Him, and of the transforming work being done by His Spirit living within her.

And then I spent what spare time I had over the next three years mining the Scriptures and studying what it means to have our *identity in Christ*—what He did for us through His death, burial, and resurrection; what He does for us day by day, month by month, year by year; and what He will do for us when we die.

My study culminated in writing a 31-day devotional, *Seeing Yourself Through God's Eyes.* The concept is simple. I thought, *If it takes 21 days to form a habit, 31 days should be long enough to form a new belief about how God views us.*

This is now our ministry's best-selling book and has been translated into more than 20 languages. Why is it so vital that we know our identity in Christ? If we don't know who we are, then we don't know our resources, we don't know our purpose, we don't know our inheritance, and we don't know our destiny. It is like living with amnesia. Just imagine not knowing who you are!

The Only Defense for Lies Is Truth

Not knowing who we are as Christians makes us easy prey for those who would fill our heads and hearts with lies about our value and worth. The only effective defense for lies is truth. If you know the truth, you will be set free from the lies and no longer live like Condemnation Carl. God loves you and established your worth by dying for you—now that is the truth!

4. No-Chance Charlie

Poor Charlie Brown. Right now, I can hear him sigh and declare, "There is no heavier burden than great potential."

Poor, frustrated Charlie—there's no chance he will succeed. He is considered the classic example of "the great American unsuccess story" because he seems to fail at everything. No one *ever* expects him to win.

It's easy to picture No-Chance Charlie standing on the pitcher's mound with his well-worn baseball cap and glove and a forlorn look in his eyes. Everyone who's read the *Peanuts* comic strip knows why this scene is so poignant—Charlie Brown has never won a game. His potential for greatness is still only an abstract possibility.

Maybe you know how that feels. Most of us approach life with great expectations of ourselves and the possibility of grand accomplishments that lie ahead. Potential is a powerful force that can indeed propel us to do great things.

But what happens when, like Charlie Brown, you feel you simply can't achieve? When the very dreams that lifted you skyward have now become a burdensome weight pulling you down?

Many people—along with Charlie—get angry about that.

They don't have the wealth they wished for, the house they hoped for, the recognition they reached for, the love they longed for, the position they prayed for, the years they yearned for. Their teenagers are in trouble, their marriage is miserable, and their physical health is failing.

So…they blame themselves. *What's wrong with me? How could I have squandered my potential?*

The fact is, life happens! And you are to yield your will to God's will—to let your plans be based on His plans, which have nothing to do with earthly accumulations, accolades, and achievements.

When His purpose includes hardship and disappointment—as it so often does—the Bible tells us to consider ourselves fortunate because reward is coming: "Blessed is the man who perseveres under trial, because when he has stood the test, he will receive the crown of life that God has promised to those who love him."[3]

Although No-Chance Charlie is considered a loveable loser, there's nothing loveable in God's eyes about always losing. In fact, God intends for us to utilize the gifts and talents He has given us, and then leave the results to Him. He desires for us to offer our potential in humble service to Him, not to live a life characterized by angry self-recrimination.

Your Value to God: He Paid the Ultimate Price for You

My brother's family was excited about moving into their new home. The carpet was down, the curtains were up, and the furniture was in. Only a few remaining items needed to be moved.

Then in the early morning, just before the family was to take up residence, a fire broke out and their possessions went up in flames. Personal items, precious mementos, and priceless pictures—all were lost.

When I arrived at the house's charred frame, I had expected to see Ray and Nancy Ann. Instead, to my horror, I learned they had gone to the homes of two firemen who had lost their lives in the blaze. The cry of all our hearts was, *If only they could have been saved!*

Only against such a tragic backdrop can we fully grasp the significance of the salvation God has provided for us.

Firefighters especially understand the gravity of life and death—of what it means to be saved.

Saved...who wouldn't want to be *saved*? Obviously, the word *saved* implies being saved *from something*. If only every person could comprehend what Scripture says they can be saved from: a present life of emptiness, the void of not being all that God created them to be, and a future destiny of fiery, eternal torment. Who wouldn't want to be rescued from such a destiny?

Recently I visited the fire station at Love Field Airport in Dallas, Texas, to learn what is necessary to know in order to save lives. Jay (the husband of one of our former ministry team members) and his fellow firefighters shared numerous points that can be applied to spiritual salvation.

Specifically I asked, "What is most important for firefighters?" Immediately, a firefighter named Langley responded, "Safety training."

The truth is, we all need to know the ultimate safety plan—from God's point of view.

What Is God's Safety Plan?

God has a plan and a purpose for us. He says, "I know the plans I have for you...plans to prosper you and not to harm you, plans to give you hope and a future."[4] Unfortunately, we have all chosen to go against God's perfect plan. This is what the Bible calls sin.

Firefighters say: "Our number one enemy is not fire, not heat, but toxic gases!"

Sin is the equivalent of toxic fumes—deadly. The word *sin* refers to anything outside of God's perfect will—both in attitude and action. Interestingly, the letter *i* is the middle letter of the word *sin*—as in, "*I* am going to do what *I* want to do when *I* want to do it." Sin, simply put, is living independently of God.

Firefighters say: "Don't get separated from your partner."

The problem with sin is this: The Bible says sin *separates* us from God. "Your [sins] have separated you from your God."[5] The Bible also says we've all sinned and fallen short of God's standard of perfection.[6] Most people want to live in heaven, but that's impossible when our sin separates us from God.

Firefighters say: "Our greatest pain is failing to save someone's life."

The firefighters shared this scripture with me: "Be merciful to those who doubt; snatch others from the fire and save them; to others show mercy, mixed with fear—hating even the clothing stained by corrupted flesh" (Jude 22-23).

But here we all have another problem: The Bible says the payment for our sin is "death."[7] Not only physical death but spiritual death, which means eternal separation from God. Now, God doesn't want us separated from Him. He says His desire is that none should perish.[8] He even provided the solution—John 3:16 says, "God so loved the world that he gave his one and only Son, that whoever believes in him shall not perish but have eternal life."

Firefighters say: "Our proudest moment is saving someone's life."

Like a firefighter, Jesus is our Savior, our Rescuer. He can save anyone from the flames...and the fumes. That is the *why* of Jesus Christ. He came literally to die on the cross to pay the penalty you would otherwise have to pay for your sins.[9] (By the way, Jesus didn't die a victim... He said, "No one takes it [My life] from me," and "[I] give [my] life as a ransom for many.")[10]

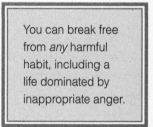

You can break free from *any* harmful habit, including a life dominated by inappropriate anger.

Jesus, who is God, came to earth and lived a perfect life. He chose to take our sins—past, present, and future—onto Himself at the cross and then rose again three days later. If we humble our hearts and ask Him to come into our lives as our Lord and Savior, giving Him control of our lives, He will forgive us of *all* our sins.

Firefighters say: "Don't stop a firefighter from doing his job."

When it comes to tearing down your wall or hacking through your door, the firefighter's way is right.

Realize that Jesus' death is the *only* sacrifice that could open up the way to eternal life. He said, "I am the way and the truth and the life. No one comes to the Father except through me."[11] God created us to spend eternity with Him. This is the eternal benefit that results from our decision to accept Christ's offer of salvation. And the amazing fact is that this salvation is a *free* gift—but it is not cheap, for it cost Christ His life. Salvation is free because He paid for it.

Firefighters say: "Close the door on the fire."

When you are fleeing a room that is on fire, close the door behind you.

Jesus will empower you to close the door on your anger.[12] Simply put, it doesn't matter what negative patterns you've developed from the past. You can break free from *any* harmful habit, including a life dominated by inappropriate anger. And that's not all. When you are in heaven, you will be forever "saved" from the very presence of sin.

Firefighters say: "Put the wet on the red."

"Put the wet on the red" means aim the hose at the hottest part of the fire.

Jesus knows how to put living water on your red-hot anger. He said, "Whoever believes in me, as the Scripture has said, streams of living water will flow from within him."[13]

It is Jesus living through you who enables real and lasting victory over anger.

Firefighters say: "Stop, drop, and roll."

If you are on fire, don't run, because you will fan the flames. You are to stop, drop, and roll. God wants you to cease your self-effort and simply stop and accept His gift of salvation. If you believe Jesus

Christ is the risen Son of God and are willing to receive Him as your personal Lord and Savior...

- *Stop!* Stop running (your own life). The Bible says, "Come back to your senses as you ought, and stop sinning; for there are some who are ignorant of God."[14]

- *Drop!* Bow your head; humble your heart. "Humble yourselves before the Lord, and he will lift you up."[15]

- *Roll!* Roll away the stone guarding your heart and give Jesus control of your life. He said, "I will give them an undivided heart and put a new spirit in them; I will remove from them their heart of stone and give them a heart of flesh."[16]

If you believe God is leading you to enter into a life-changing relationship with Him, you can do that right now by praying, expressing what's in your heart...

My Salvation Prayer

"God, I want a real relationship with You.
I admit that many times I've chosen to
go my own way instead of Your way.
Please forgive me for my sins.
Jesus, thank You for dying on the cross to pay the penalty
for my sins and for rising from the grave.
Come into my life to be my Lord and my Savior.
I give You control of my life.
Change me from the inside out and make me the person
You created me to be.
In Your holy name I pray. Amen."

If you sincerely prayed this prayer, look at what Jesus says has happened to you: "Whoever hears my word and believes him who sent me has eternal life and will not be condemned; he has crossed over from death to life."[17]

God never intended for you to live apart from Him for eternity or to be consumed by the punishing flames of anger. Jesus paid the ultimate price so that you can be forever free, saved, healed, and whole. Only a God of boundless love can give us a life of such beauty in exchange for our ashes.[18]

Fuming at the Father

How Assumptions About God Result in Bitter Anger

> *"People ruin their lives by their own foolishness*
> *and then are angry at the LORD"*
> (PROVERBS 19:3 NLT).

THE NEWSPAPER HEADLINE caught my eye: "Man 'Angry at God' Drives Minivan into Church Sanctuary." The article began:

> A man who said he was angry at God drove a minivan through a Catholic church in Rancho Cordova, California, late on Saturday night. Harold David Zequeda, 36, drove a silver Ford Windstar through St. John Vianney Church. Witnesses said the driver pulled onto the church's front lawn and floored the gas pedal.[1]

The van broke through a set of locked steel doors and then a second set of heavy wooden doors. The vehicle then collided with a 100-pound communion table, propelling it across the sanctuary. The car traveled 50 yards across the church, slamming into solid-oak pews and stopping just short of a statue of Jesus.

Amazingly, no one was injured in the incident.

Why would this man do something so extreme? Here's a mysterious clue: Police were told that the driver dropped a photograph of several young children and was angry at God.

"It seemed like a cry for help," said the church's priest, Father Martin Moroney. "I just wish he had cried out in some other way."

Zequeda was charged with vandalizing a house of worship—a felony—and driving with a suspended license. He was held on a million dollars bail.

We might shake our heads at this man's behavior, but most of us can relate to his feelings of being upset, disappointed, or even angry with God. As I've spoken with thousands of people across the country, I've learned that many have felt anger toward God. Thankfully, most of us do not act on our feelings by smashing vehicles into churches. But our anger, if left unresolved, can be damaging in other ways.

When we feel hurt or victimized or unjustly treated, we naturally feel angry. We want to do something with those fiery feelings—we want to blame someone, we want recompense or revenge, and we want answers as to why this happened. If there is no one else to point fingers at, God serves as a convenient scapegoat, and we blame God for our anger.

God's Anger—a Mystery

Most of us would rather not think about God's wrath. Imagining God as angry can create contradictions in our view of Him that we are hard-pressed to resolve. This is especially true when we view anger only as an evil, savage emotion associated with slammed doors, shattered hearts, and splintered relationships. If anger is always a bad thing, how can we comprehend a loving God who gets angry?

> The Bible teaches us that anger is every bit as much a part of God's character as mercy and forgiveness.

Our resistance to the idea is understandable. Anyone who has a truly intimate relationship with God knows the joy of basking in the warm glow of His fatherly affection and the peace of sleeping securely in His fatherly protection.

He invites us, like children, to abandon our cares and climb onto His lap, where we may rest in His reassuring arms. There, by His infinite grace, we are surrounded with love. It's hard to imagine that He is also a thundering, fiery God.

The Lord says to us, "I have loved you with an everlasting love; I have drawn you with loving-kindness" (Jeremiah 31:3).

This is all true, every word. God's love is everlasting; His faithfulness is never ending. The confusion arises when we stop there and believe that's all there is to God's nature. We could simply ignore the whole issue if it weren't for Scripture passages that describe God's anger at His people because of their stubborn and rebellious hearts:

- "Because they have forsaken me...my anger will burn against this place" (2 Kings 22:17).
- "When the LORD heard them, he was very angry...for they did not believe in God or trust in his deliverance" (Psalm 78:21-22).

There's no getting around it: The Bible teaches us that anger is every bit as much a part of God's character as mercy and forgiveness. At times, even Jesus got angry and didn't hesitate to openly—even heatedly—express it. So, what does all this mean?

Is it possible that in trying to eradicate anger entirely we have unintentionally declared war on a natural emotion that can be extremely useful, and even godly? Absolutely—the answer is *yes*.

Our God gets angry—but *righteously* angry. Would we really want it any other way? Can you imagine God as One who loves evil, abuse, rape, and incest? We want our God to *hate* evil as a motivation to further the cause of justice.

Are You Angry at God?

Problems, pain, and perplexities—you can't escape them. But do you blame God for the heartache in your life? Have you pointed a condemning finger and pronounced judgment on Him because He has not stopped evil or suffering? Or because He has not stopped you from making bad decisions?

Periodically I am asked: "I'm angry at God for allowing bad people to cause so much pain. If God had the power to create the world, why doesn't He stop evil in the world?"

An understandable question! The plain and simple truth is God allows evil because He allows people to exercise free will. He did not create us to be robots with no choice or to do only what the Creator programmed.

God created us to be free-agent human beings who have choice over what we think, say, and do. We can't have it both ways—we can't have God allowing us freedom yet preventing us from doing wrong— that's not freedom.

If you have read the last book of the Bible, Revelation, you know God has appointed a time in the future when He will put an end to evil and suffering. The bad news is, until then, evil will always be in opposition to good and will seek to harm and destroy those who love God.

But the good news is God always turns evil around and uses it to accomplish His purposes. He did so in the life of Joseph, a prominent character in the Bible, whose evil brothers sold him into slavery. Years later, when the frightened brothers came face-to-face with Joseph— now a prime minister of Egypt who had saved both the Egyptians and Hebrews from famine—he said, "Don't be afraid. Am I in the place of God? You intended to harm me, but God intended it for good to accomplish what is now being done, the saving of many lives" (Genesis 50:19-20).

An Old, Old Lesson

In the Old Testament of the Bible we find the story of Job, one of the greatest tales of suffering ever recorded. The Lord highly honored Job before Satan, saying, "There is no one on earth like him; he is blameless and upright, a man who fears God and shuns evil" (Job 1:8).

Satan's response was to challenge God concerning the faithfulness of His choice servant when under pressure—*intense* pressure. Satan's supposition? If incredibly blessed and righteous Job were thrown into a fiery furnace of affliction, he would rise up and curse God. And so a supernatural showdown ensued.

God allowed Satan to take away Job's wealth, family, and health— everything except his very life (and his wife). Understandably, Job felt unjustly singled out for catastrophe and cried out, "God has turned me over to evil men and thrown me into the clutches of the wicked. All was well with me, but he shattered me; he seized me by the neck and crushed me. He has made me his target" (Job 16:11-12).

How many of us have thought something similar? *Everything was going just fine, but then God caused all these terrible things to happen.*

Job did not understand why God would allow such tragedy in his life. "Even today my complaint is bitter; his hand is heavy in spite of my groaning. If only I knew where to find him; if only I could go to his dwelling! I would state my case before him and fill my mouth with arguments."[2]

Although our pain and suffering probably will never approach what Job endured, we echo his questions and share his feelings. When painful events befall us, we feel confused, abandoned, and aggrieved. Where is God in the midst of our pain? Doesn't He care? Why doesn't He stop this? Hasn't He noticed our deep despair, the tear-stained slips in our anger bowl...*with His name on them?*

Can We Share Our Angry Feelings with God?

You might be wondering if it's okay to have poignant questions for God or to feel anger toward Him. Many people I speak with preface their comments by saying, "I know I shouldn't feel mad at God, but..." It is my belief that anger toward God can be an understandable response when pain penetrates our lives.

We are in a relationship with the Father, and in every honest, authentic relationship there will be conflicts, tension, and misunderstandings. We may, indeed, find ourselves "fuming at the Father." God can handle our anger. He doesn't turn a deaf ear to our "why" questions, nor does He distance Himself from our heartache and pain.

Misconceptions and Misplaced Anger

However—and this is a *big* however—I also believe anger toward God is *misplaced anger.* This is true each and every time—no exceptions. The Bible tells us over and over that God is just, holy, loving, perfect, and compassionate. He *always* has our best interests in mind, He *always* wants what is good for us, and He *always* grieves along with us when we hurt. So when we feel anger toward God, it is because we have forgotten or misunderstood His character.

As I've listened to many struggling people tell me about their anger toward God, I've noticed their feelings typically revolve around a cluster of questions:

Why is God silent?

Why doesn't He answer my prayer? Why didn't God intervene and help me?

Why do bad people get away with doing evil? Where's the justice? Why doesn't God protect and bless believers more than unbelievers?

When people ask these questions, it's because they feel neglected, slighted, or even cheated by God. They think He broke His part of the "bargain."

"God, I'll do my part, and You do Yours."

That's the way it works, they think, because the Bible is filled with promises for protection, prosperity, guidance, and deliverance. What happens, then, when God doesn't *seem* to be there or doesn't *appear* to be keeping His promises? People feel disappointed, deflated, disillusioned.

Our heart tells us one thing (God doesn't care about me), while our mind says the opposite (God cares deeply about me). We know intellectually that the Lord is faithful and just, but our emotions may lead us to believe He looks the other way when we experience hurt, injustice, fear, and frustration, and He simply leaves us to fend for ourselves.

It's vital to realize that our anger toward God will not bring us any closer to finding peace, overcoming pain, or resolving problems. So, what can we do? Consider Denise's story...

Pour Your Heart Out to Him

Denise called me on *Hope In The Night*, saying she was angry at God for the loss of her beloved 12-year-old daughter, Madeline, who had died of cancer the year before.

Although Denise had enjoyed a close walk with the Lord for years, after her daughter's death she had to force herself, with every ounce of willpower, to attend church, read the Bible, and pray.

I asked if she had told the Lord why she was angry and shared her feelings with Him.

"Oh, no! I couldn't do that! I ask for His strength and pray for the health of my other children, but that's about it."

"Why wouldn't you share your true feelings with Him?"

"I guess I've always been taught to be respectful and reverent when talking with God," she said. "He's perfect and holy…and that's how I'm supposed to be, too."

This sincere woman got part of the equation right—we *are* to approach God with respect. But we are also encouraged to be completely open with Him, even when our sentiments are not all sweet and happy. God is an excellent listener, and He invites us to pour out our hearts to Him.

Like Denise, some people are hesitant, fearing lightning bolts from heaven if they speak openly—much less *angrily*—to God. We can, however, be direct without being disrespectful, blunt without being blasphemous. We can admit we have an anger bowl without hurling it up toward heaven.

Above all, God desires a *relationship* with His children, and a genuine relationship is impossible without honest communication.

Get Clear About God's Character

To get to the heart of Denise's heartache, I knew my conversation with her would need to delve directly into the character of God. It is our perceptions about God's character that influence everything we think and do.

June: "Sometimes when we encounter trials, a voice down deep whispers: 'Maybe God isn't as trustworthy as He says. Surely if God loved me, He wouldn't have let this happen.' Have you ever heard that voice?"

Denise: "There hasn't been a day since Madeline died that I *don't* hear that voice. I hate it…I try to ignore it…but it's there."

June: "I understand, Denise. And, more importantly, God understands, too. In the Garden of Eden, the serpent said to Eve, 'Did God really say, "You must not eat from any tree in the garden?"'[3] Eve responded that God said she and Adam could eat from any tree except for the one in the middle of the garden. If they ate of that tree, they would die.

"But the serpent, who is Satan's instrument, scoffed and said, 'You will not surely die…For God knows that when you eat of it your eyes will be opened, and you will be like God, knowing good and evil.'[4] Satan said, in essence, that God was lying; He was trying to trick you; He can't be trusted. And the rest, as they say, is history.

"Could Satan be using this tragedy to drive a wedge between you and your heavenly Father?"

Denise: "I see what you're saying. It's like Satan is whispering lies to harden my heart."

June: "Exactly! He is crafty enough to prey upon us when we're most vulnerable. Even so, we can't pin everything on Satan. Often our own doubts, fragile faith, and wounded emotions can cause us to wonder if Christianity is all it's cracked up to be, or if God is really who He claims to be. That's when we must remind ourselves of what the Bible says about God. We need to solidify what we know about His character. In fact, let's take a moment and do that right now. Tell me, Denise: What are some aspects of God's character that mean the most to you?"

> When we truly understand who God is…it will be impossible to stay angry at Him for long.

Denise: "Probably the most important thing to me is His love."

June: "Excellent! He is loving! Romans 8:38-39 says, 'I am convinced that neither death nor life, neither angels nor demons, neither the present nor the future, nor any powers, neither height nor depth, nor anything else in all creation, will be able to separate us from the love of God that is in Christ Jesus our Lord.' What else do we know about God's character?"

Denise: "I know He doesn't change. The summer before Madeline died, she and I memorized a scripture together: 'Every good and perfect gift is from above, coming down from the Father of the heavenly lights, who does not change like shifting shadows.'"[5]

June: "That's beautiful. Yes! God doesn't change. His character is the same yesterday, today, and forever. What a comfort it is to know that, unlike us, God's perfect character is perfectly constant."

Denise and I continued recounting the virtues of God's character—how, in addition to being loving and unchangeable, the Bible assures us He is also...

> *Eager to forgive*—"If we confess our sins, he is faithful and just and will forgive us our sins and purify us from all unrighteousness."[6]
>
> *Merciful*—"The LORD is gracious and righteous, our God is full of compassion."[7]
>
> *Sovereign*—"He does as he pleases with the powers of heaven and the peoples of the earth. No one can hold back his hand."[8]

As we considered the wonderful attributes of God, I shared my conviction that when we truly understand who God is—and realize His impeccable character can never be compromised—it will be impossible to stay angry at Him for long.

Before hanging up the phone that night I prayed with Denise, asking God to replace her anger with reassurance of His perfect love and plan for her life. I also sent her our resource titled, *Evil and Suffering...Why?*

I had no reason to believe I'd ever hear from Denise again, but I was wrong. The following year, I received this touching note:

> Dear June,
>
> While figuratively pounding my fists against my heavenly Father's chest and becoming exhausted to the point of surrender, I discovered an incredible aspect of His unfailing love. Standing there emotionally spent and still—before Him—I became aware of His heart...and despite my misdirected anger toward Him, eventually I began to feel His gentle strength... and the security of His tender embrace.
>
> Thank you, June, for helping me see, finally, that God was never to blame for Madeline's death, and that, no matter what happens from here on in my life, His character is my assurance that I can always trust Him.

As for me, it was not hard to imagine the Father gently cleansing every last bit of ashen residue and preparing this special woman to share her newfound hope with other grieving mothers in the months and years to come.

Trust the Judge to Bring Justice

As we've seen, one of the biggest causes of anger can be summed up in a word: injustice. We want to know the wrongdoer will be punished, the criminal will be sent to prison, and the bully will get his comeuppance. So we cry out to God, "You're not going to let him get away with that, are You?" We get mad at the Lord when our offender seems to get off scot-free.

I understand this struggle very well because a desire for justice seems to be hardwired into my DNA. For many years of my Christian life, I preferred the Old Testament version of justice ("an eye for an eye, a tooth for a tooth") to the New Testament version, in which Jesus seems to forgive sinners "too easily." Where was the justice?

Then one day it was as if the Spirit spoke to me: "You, too, are living in the era of Jesus' grace and mercy." It dawned on me that I, too, am the recipient of God's compassion, and that He has not dealt with me in the way I deserve. I wouldn't want to incur His wrath and judgment, so was it right to wish that upon others?

But there's more. God *is* just, and He has promised to mete out justice in His time, in His way. Here's what He has told us:

- "It is mine to avenge; I will repay. In due time their foot will slip; their day of disaster is near and their doom rushes upon them" (Deuteronomy 32:35).

- "Will not God bring about justice for his chosen ones, who cry out to him day and night? Will he keep putting them off? I tell you, he will see that they get justice, and quickly" (Luke 18:7-8).

Jesus Himself provides an example for us to help us trust God with matters of justice: "When they hurled their insults at him, he did not retaliate; when he suffered, he made no threats. Instead, he entrusted himself to him who judges justly" (1 Peter 2:23). It's up to God, the divine Judge, to ensure justice—and He will. It's up to us to trust Him to deliver on His promises.

Recognize Pain Has a Purpose

Anger and pain go hand in hand. Some pain is a mere twinge, some is like a sledgehammer to the skull. Some is short-lived, some seems to last forever.

Over the years, I have counseled many pain-filled people. Most of them have asked the same anguished question: "Why did God let this happen?" We still think pain is random and pointless. We beg God to take it away—*right now*. That's okay. Most people are surprised and encouraged when I remind them that Jesus did the very same thing.

Just after the Last Supper, the Lord went with His disciples to pray in the Garden of Gethsemane. Although His followers were still pretty clueless about what was coming, Jesus knew He would soon be arrested and put on trial. It didn't matter that He was entirely blameless; it didn't matter that He had been set up. He foresaw the pain, humiliation, and horrible death that awaited Him, and He was gripped with anguish.

Despite being the Son of God and having all the resources of heaven and earth available to Him, the prospect of His imminent crucifixion was almost more than even He could bear. He told Peter and the others, "'My soul is very sorrowful, even to death. Remain here and watch.' And going a little farther, he fell on the ground and prayed that, if it were possible, the hour might pass from him...'Abba, Father, all things are possible for you. Remove this cup from me.'"[9]

That sounds like something you and I might pray: "Make this problem go away; get rid of this illness; take these struggles off my shoulders." Yet Jesus knew something that escapes most of us when we are crippled by pain and angry because of it: He understood His suffering had a purpose. As much as He wished to be spared, He saw the incomparable good God would bring out of the incomprehensible injustice of His death. So even though His sweat fell to the ground like great drops of blood, He earnestly prayed, "Yet, not my will, but yours be done."[10]

꙳

If you are in pain, the right question to ask isn't "Why?" but "How?" "How, Lord? How are You going to use this tough situation to shape my character and deepen my faith? How are You going to accomplish Your will through this ordeal?"

Then, follow in Jesus' steps and pray for God's will to be done, knowing that "in all things God works for the good of those who love him, who have been called according to his purpose."[11] Did you catch that? *All* things.

Part Three

Fighting Fire with Fire:

How to Use Anger in Healthy Ways

Smoldering Embers

How to Extinguish the Pain of Unresolved Anger

> *"A quarrelsome person starts fights*
> *as easily as hot embers light charcoal or fire lights wood"*
> (PROVERBS 26:21 NLT).

I FIRST MET Vivian one evening after I'd given a seminar on how to resolve persistent anger. She had the panicked look of a woman whose emotional thermostat was set too high.

"I came tonight because I thought I might get some insight into my husband's behavior when he loses his temper," she told me. "But something unexpected happened—I saw *myself* in what you said."

Vivian's "Aha!" moment came when I spoke of unresolved anger hanging around for so long we've stopped even being consciously aware of its presence. The fireworks no longer light up the sky, so we think they've burned themselves out. But that's not the case. The emotional pyrotechnics have simply headed underground, boring deep into unguarded areas of our hearts, minds, and emotions, where they continue to smolder indefinitely.

Such anger still singes us—and others—but in subtle ways that are difficult to trace to the original source.

"I knew you were talking about me," continued Vivian, a look of anguish on her face. "After all these years, my anger suddenly surfaced. Why haven't I seen it before now?"

I began to understand as she told more of her story. As a little girl,

Vivian loved to bake breads and pastries. By the time she was in high school, she frequently sent her mother out of the kitchen and prepared desserts for the family by herself. She knew she had found her calling and dreamed of one day running her own bakery.

Vivian's sister, Lorraine, was her polar opposite. While Vivian was creative and spontaneous, Lorraine was serious and sensible. Everyone said she had a head for business.

It was as if God had provided a perfect partnership for success all in one family: Vivian could work the kitchen, and Lorraine could manage the business.

The sisters made a pact to open a neighborhood bakery as soon as Lorraine finished college. But after only two years, Lorraine grew impatient.

She felt well-enough equipped to dive into the real world of commerce and get on with it. Lorraine dropped out of school and, through family connections, the sisters found a financial backer for their enterprise. Six months later, they opened a stylish bakery and breakfast bistro in a good location.

"My dream had come true," Vivian recalled. "I pinched myself every time I saw a line of customers stretching all the way to the door."

A Recipe for Financial Disaster

But after a few months, the dream abruptly exploded like the grand finale at a fireworks display. While Vivian held up her end of the bargain—creating delicious food attracting loyal customers—Lorraine was quietly making a mess of hers. She was in way over her head, drowning in the details of the day-to-day financial management of a burgeoning business. Rather than seeking help, she grew even more rash and reckless in her decisions.

"By the time I knew there was a problem," Vivian said, "our operating capital was gone and we were deeply in debt to our suppliers. In the end, we couldn't pay the bills or the staff, and bankruptcy was our only option."

"How awful that must have been for you," I commented.

"I was devastated," Vivian replied. "It was like watching a loved one die."

"And I imagine you were pretty angry at Lorraine for what she had done," I said.

"Absolutely," she responded. "But there wasn't really time to dwell on it or address it."

That's because, as painful as the bankruptcy was for Vivian, it hit Lorraine like a blazing fireball. Realizing it was her fault the business failed, she turned to alcohol and sank into a deep depression lasting several years.

Vivian, alarmed by her sister's emotional frailty, worked almost single-handedly to repay their remaining debts. Even after Lorraine's condition improved, Vivian never mentioned the catastrophe for fear of being "too judgmental" and pushing her sister back into self-destructive behavior.

> The road to forgiveness leads *through* our anger, not around it, as if it had never existed in the first place.

"I felt that was what God wanted of me—to just forgive and forget," she said through her tears. "I was so hurt and so mad, but I did what I had to do to force my anger to go away." Or so she thought. What caused Vivian pain in the present was the dawning realization that her past anger had never really gone away at all.

That then affected many of Vivian's subsequent relationships—with her husband, whom she had difficulty trusting; with her children, who often accused her of being hypercritical; and with all her other bosses and business partners.

Vivian had genuinely tried to do the right thing by letting bygones be bygones. But in the process, she forgot an inescapable truth: The road to forgiveness leads *through* our anger, not around it, as if it had never existed in the first place.

Seven Steps to Peace and Freedom

Twenty years had since gone by and Vivian feared it was too late to overcome her anger and repair the widespread damage it had caused. She worried it had become an inseparable, incurable part of her personality.

Fortunately, she was wrong. I reminded her nothing is beyond God's ability or willingness to heal. I told her God could help her begin anew. Listen to what the Lord says in Isaiah 43:18-19:

> *"Forget the former things; do not dwell on the past.*
> *See, I am doing a new thing! Now it springs up; do you not perceive it?*
> *I am making a way in the desert and streams in the wasteland."*

I told Vivian, "I know it is overwhelming to rummage through past pain. But time is no barrier at all to God's capacity to repair what is broken."

So as long as we are willing to place our trust in God—and do everything we can to help extinguish the smoldering coals—we can resolve our anger, no matter how old it is. Here's how:

1. Realize You Are Still Angry

You can't possibly hope to resolve your anger until you acknowledge it exists. That sounds simple, but for many of us the hardest words we ever say are, "I feel hurt, frustrated, and angry."

It can be difficult enough to express how we feel in the heat of the moment, when there is still an obvious link between cause and effect. So how much more difficult does it become when the original source of our anger is years or even decades old?

Oh, get over it! we say to ourselves accusingly. *Are you still steamed about that? Just put it behind you and move on.*

Contrary to the popular cliché, time does *not* heal all wounds. It may appear to turn down the temperature, but our anger still burns. The "sleeping dogs" you've been taught to let lie aren't really asleep and are not better left alone. Even the most long-ago unresolved anger will manifest itself in your life—through bitterness, chronic depression, lack of trust, and a defensive, hostile stance in your relationships.

Warning Signs of Hidden Anger

Do you recognize any of these warning signs of hidden anger in your life?

- Do you feel uncomfortable in someone's company, even years later?
- Do you find it difficult to sincerely pray for someone?
- Do you have bitter jealousy of another's successes?
- Do you hope for the worst, instead of the best, for someone?
- Do you secretly find pleasure in someone's defeats?
- Do you take part in critical gossip about someone (or at least do nothing to stop it)?
- Do you become irritable over trifles?
- Do you smile on the outside while you hurt or rage on the inside?
- Do you find your identity and worth in excessive work?
- Do you deny ever being impatient or frustrated?
- Do you have to have the last word?
- Do those close to you say you blame others?
- Do you feel emotionally flat?
- Do you have a loss of interest in life?
- Do you experience physical manifestations—a queasy feeling, clenched stomach muscles, racing heart, and so on—when you think about a particular person or situation?

If any of these describe how you feel, chances are your anger is not as resolved as you had hoped. Don't despair. God knows exactly where you've hidden your pain and rage. Ask Him to pull back the covering of time and show it to you as well—then own up to it. Admit you are still angry so the healing process can finally begin.

2. Reckon with Your Anger Pie

Have you ever comprehensively considered *how much* anger you are holding inside your heart and *toward whom* you feel angry? If not, I invite you to create your very own Anger Pie. (No baking required!) I've found it to be an amazingly effective tool for surfacing buried anger. Here's how to make it:

- Make a list of people toward whom you have had anger (from childhood to present).

- Draw a circle—pie-shaped—that represents all of the anger in your life.

- Divide your pie into different-sized wedges. Base the size of each wedge on the size of your anger toward each person on your list.

I've provided a sample Anger Pie for you,[1] using general categories. As you process your anger constructively, you will see the size of your slices shrinking. That's a good indication you are working effectively through your anger issues.

The Anger Pie

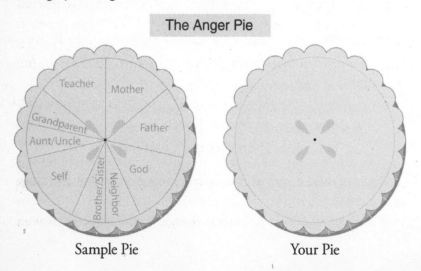

Sample Pie   Your Pie

3. Revisit Your Reasons for Being Angry

Imagine experiencing two months of terrible stomach pains and severe headaches. Your energy is depleted most of the time, as if your batteries were being continually drained.

Initially you tell yourself, *That's just life.* But finally, you concede the symptoms are not normal. You're forced to admit something is wrong.

Of course, realizing you are sick is a huge step on the road to wellness. But would you stop there? Most likely, you would want to know the answer to the obvious: Why am I feeling so sick? And you would want to seek a doctor's help because you understand finding a *cure* for your ailments requires knowing the *cause*.

The same is true of anger that is plaguing you. Once you have admitted you're still angry at someone for a past offense, it is necessary to sift through the debris like an arson investigator. Which of the four causes inflames you: hurt, injustice, fear, or frustration…or a combination of two or more of these causes? (See chapter 3.)

What are the triggers that ignite your "smoldering embers"? What were the combustible ingredients? What are the traces of flammable residue? What caused the sparks to fly? In short, why did this thing explode?

This is dangerous work. After all, poking around in hot embers can stoke the flames of fury. Chances are, that's why you've ignored the suppressed heat for so long. It's safer to "stuff it" than expose it to a fresh supply of emotional oxygen and risk a raging inferno that might consume your relationships. But if you hope to put out the fire once and for all, it is a necessary risk.

For one thing, time can act like a magnifying glass by making painful offenses seem larger when we look back at them from a distance. Our wounds can seem more grievous and our enemies can seem more evil. But by revisiting "the scene of the crime" with an open mind and a heart bent on healing, we can remove the distortion and see things in proper perspective.

What's more, human conflict is rarely a clear-cut battle between "the good guys" and "the bad guys." Nearly every time I look back on an angry skirmish with someone in my life, I see things *I* did to fan the flames or at least keep things boiling longer than necessary.

Vivian discovered that very thing in herself when she examined her anger toward her sister. She had to admit there were plenty of warning signs showing Lorraine was in trouble, if only she'd been willing to notice them.

"Every day she grew more sullen and withdrawn," Vivian recalled. "But I was happier than I'd ever been and didn't want to be pulled down by her gloominess. I never once asked if she was okay or needed help."

Gaining an honest and accurate perspective of what really happened—and taking responsibility for the part we may have played—begins to douse the smoldering coals and prepares us for the next step toward resolving our anger.

4. Release Those Who Have Wronged You

If we wish to be free of past anger, there is a key question we must ask ourselves: Whom have I not yet forgiven?

Anger doesn't materialize out of thin air. This strong emotion naturally arises when someone's actions cause us to feel hurt, afraid, frustrated, or offended at an injustice. Anger can be a constructive response to anything that threatens us. But it quickly becomes *destructive* when we hang on to our fears and wounds and refuse to forgive those who cause them.

Why should I forgive? we think. *I'm the one who was wronged!*

Yet as hard as it is, God has commanded us to forgive each other and even made it a condition for our own forgiveness. We can't expect to receive a benefit from Him that we have stubbornly withheld from another. As Jesus told His disciples: "When you stand praying, if you hold anything against anyone,

> If we refuse to forgive, we are taking on the role of being a higher judge than God Himself!

forgive him, so that your Father in heaven may forgive you your sins"
(Mark 11:25).

Here are a number of helpful thoughts concerning forgiveness: First,
forgiving someone is not the same as condoning offensive behavior. It
is unfortunate many of us have the habit of saying, "It's okay" when
what we mean is, "I forgive you." Saying that an offense is okay mistakenly implies it is no big deal. But it's never okay when you've been
unjustly hurt by someone.

Some people sincerely but mistakenly assume that if they forgive
an offender, they must reestablish the relationship. Unfortunately, this
mistaken assumption has kept countless victims from forgiving their
victimizers. Very simply, forgiveness is not the same as reconciliation.

- Forgiveness can take place with only one person; reconciliation requires at least two people.
- Forgiveness is a free gift to the one who has broken trust; reconciliation is a restored relationship based on restored trust.
- Forgiveness is extended even if it is never, ever earned; reconciliation is offered to the offender because it has been earned.
- Forgiveness is unconditional, regardless of a lack of repentance; reconciliation is conditional based on repentance.

Many other misconceptions abound about forgiveness. Often people
won't forgive because they don't "feel like it." But forgiveness is not a
feeling, it is a choice—an act of the will. Also:

- *Forgiveness is not* based on what is fair. It was not fair for Jesus
  to hang on the cross, but He did so that we could be forgiven.
- *Forgiveness is not* being a weak martyr. It is being strong
  enough to be Christlike.
- *Forgiveness is not* letting the guilty off the hook. It is moving
  the guilty from your hook to God's hook.

Why Should We Forgive?

We are called to forgive others because that is precisely what Jesus came to earth to do for us. He died on the cross so that our sins would be forgiven. Likewise, He tells us to forgive our offenders. Therefore, if we refuse to forgive, we are taking on the role of being a higher judge than God Himself!

Second, as author William Walton vividly described it, "To carry a grudge is like being stung to death by one bee."[2] What a picture! In other words, just one grudge can eventually debilitate us.

Angry unforgiveness harms you just as much, if not more, than the one who hurt you. It binds you to your pain and perpetuates your anger. To forgive by releasing your resentment is to free yourself as well.

How Do You Actually Forgive Someone?

Make a list of all your offender's offenses—they are your "rocks" of resentment. Imagine a meat hook around your neck. Then imagine a burlap bag filled with your heavy rocks of resentment hanging from the hook. Everywhere you go, this heavy burden weighs you down. Ask yourself: *Do I really want to carry all this pain the rest of my life?* (Obviously not!)

Are you willing to take your offender and the offenses off your emotional hook and put this person and all the pain onto God's hook? The Lord knows how to handle it all, in His time and in His way. Deuteronomy 32:35 says, "It is mine to avenge; I will repay."

You can release your resentment right now by sincerely praying this prayer:

Forgiveness Prayer

*"Heavenly Father, thank You for caring about how much
my heart has been hurt. You know the pain I have felt
because of (list every offense). Right now I release all
that pain into Your hands. Thank You for Jesus' dying
on the cross for me and extending Your forgiveness to*

me. As an act of my will, I choose to forgive (name).
Right now, I move (name) off my emotional hook to
Your hook. I refuse all thoughts of revenge. I trust that
in Your time and in Your way You will deal with my
offender as You see fit. And Lord, thank You for giving
me Jesus' power to forgive so that I can be set free.
In Jesus' holy name I pray. Amen."

5. Replace Your Anger with Trust in God's Love

Anger is a defense mechanism. It is designed to help you avoid further pain when you've experienced something traumatic. When you stay mad for a long period of time, you can become attached—and accustomed—to your habitual anger.

That's why, when you begin to let go, it's important to fill the emotional void with a new source of comfort and security: the assurance of God's unfailing protection in your life. Whereas you once defended yourself behind a firewall of hostility, you must learn to take shelter in the invincible fortress of God's love. Not that you won't still experience attacks—fireballs will still be hurled. But never forget that God's shielding grace surrounds you.

The only fireballs that will land in your life are those God allows to get through. In that case, they are used for *your good* and *His purposes.*

Does this sound familiar? Do you have the feeling you are not the first to walk this path? If you've read the Psalms, the answer is surely *yes.* On page after page, David and other psalmists poured out their heartrending feelings of hurt, fear, frustration, and injustice—only to return time and time again to the familiar touchstone of God's infinite goodness and might. As David wrote:

"My salvation and my honor depend on God;
He is my mighty rock, my refuge…
One thing God has spoken, two things have I heard:
that you, O God, are strong,
and that you, O Lord, are loving.

Surely you will reward each person
according to what he has done"
(PSALM 62:7,11-12).

Here's a powerful path to freedom: As you learn to let go of unresolved anger, let God's Word speak to you. Read at least five psalms a
day for a month. Read them out loud, and soon peace will permeate
your mind and spirit instead of painful angst.

When I made the conscious choice to forgive my father and release
all my grievances to God, it was not because my father *asked* for forgiveness or showed any signs of remorse or repentance. It was not because
I thought he deserved it or because I knew I "should." It was because
God said, "Do it," which meant it was in my best interest.

Convinced of God's love for me and persuaded of His trustwor-
thiness, I wholeheartedly trusted His instructions to me. So for me
the choice was clear and the decision definite—it was a no-brainer. I
would do whatever God asked of me, just as Jesus did whatever the
Father asked of Him—even if it meant forgiving the guilty and trusting God with the most significant matter of justice.

Just as Jesus entrusted Himself to the Father, He asks us to entrust
ourselves to Him. And when you know you are loved unconditionally and sacrificially, it is more than doable! So as an act of my will, I
chose to forgive my father.

From all outward appearances, nothing changed. My father was
the same. Our relationship was still the same. But God knew my heart
was not the same. It had been deeply—and forever—changed.

6. Restore the Relationship When Possible

Once you have *realized* and *revisited* your buried anger, as well
as *released* the ones who hurt you from their debt, be ready to seize
the opportunity to *rebuild* the trust needed for healthy relationships.
Naturally, God's purpose is for us to live peacefully with each other
whenever possible.

The apostle Paul wrote in Romans 12:17-18, "Do not repay anyone evil for evil. Be careful to do what is right in the eyes of everybody. it is possible, as far as it depends on you, live at peace with everyone.

That is a recipe for harmony in all of our relationships. But notice a key phrase in this verse: "If it is possible, as far as it depends on you…" When it comes to restoring a broken relationship, this is the crux of the matter. Reconciliation isn't always possible or even desirable.

God doesn't expect us to "get along" no matter what.

Our protection from further harm always comes first. If the person who wronged you refuses to take responsibility for hurtful actions and shows no signs of genuine contrition, then it probably wouldn't be wise to pursue restoration of the relationship.

Again, forgiveness is a commandment. It is a volitional act of obedience to God's will. Healing from unresolved anger requires genuine determination on your part alone to cancel the debt owed you.

But reconciling a broken relationship takes two people—both need to reassemble the pieces of shattered confidence. It takes genuine repentance—a change of mind, heart, and behavior and the completion of verifiable steps to prevent a recurrence of a breakdown in trust. Both people must work toward restoring the relationship.

> The ultimate purpose of our fiery trials is to clear away everything holding us back from a more mature, more empowered walk with Christ.

Here's the bottom line: If the one who made you angry is willing to take responsibility for wrongs done and to start over, don't hesitate to do your part as well. Reconciliation pleases the heart of God.

7. Rejoice in God's Purpose

Few things on earth are more desolate than a forest after a ravaging fire has reduced it to ashes. It is easy to look at the charred stumps and think there is no hope for recovery.

But oh, how appearances can deceive! Return to the scorched area the following spring and you'll see a vivid illustration of God's ability to turn any tribulation into triumph. In relatively little time, "dead"

...ve with colorful wildflowers and green grasses. Old ... choking out the new is gone, clearing the way for ... of fresh life.

Our hearts, once laid waste by pain and anger, are no different. The ultimate purpose of our fiery trials is to clear away everything holding us back from a more mature, more empowered walk with Christ.

As the inspired apostle Paul wrote:

> *"In all these things we are more than conquerors through*
> *him who loved us. For I am convinced that neither death nor life,*
> *neither angels nor demons, neither the present nor the future,*
> *nor any powers, neither height nor depth, nor anything else*
> *in all creation, will be able to separate us from the love of God*
> *that is in Christ Jesus our Lord"*
> (ROMANS 8:37-38).

So the final step in dousing the smoldering anger inside you is to rejoice in the *good* God promises to produce out of all you've been through as you commit your trials to Him. As forgiveness douses those burning embers, begin to look for signs of new life in your own heart and soul. Look for the beauty God will bring from the ashes.

※

You Can Find Serenity After Surfacing Your Anger

Vivian called me months later to report she was making steady progress toward shedding the unnecessary burden of her unresolved anger. She and Lorraine finally talked through their past and forgave each other.

"It's like all those years I've been dragging around a 100-pound sack of potatoes," she told me. "Now with the weight lifted, I feel like a whole new person without it."

Hidden anger may be difficult to recognize, but it's definitely *felt*— by you, and by those around you. Admit it, forgive it, release it, and —like Vivian—never again drag around a 100-pound sack of potatoes!

Let Cooler Heads Prevail

How to Put Out the Flames of Present Anger

"Good sense makes one slow to anger"
(PROVERBS 19:11 ESV).

IMAGINE YOURSELF SUDDENLY thrust into one of these situations:

- At an important work meeting, someone takes credit for a big idea you've spent weeks preparing. He gets all the credit; you get none. *Grrrr!*
- Your kids have a raucous pillow fight in the living room—which they've been told not to do—and they break your most cherished, sentimental gift (the old clock passed down from your grandparents). *No!*
- Your accountant calls with bad news about an error on your tax return. With fees, penalties, and so on, you'll need to come up with an extra $7500. *What!*
- The one you love the most suddenly snaps at you, "I'm leaving! I hate you—I never want to see you again!" *Bam!*

I'm sure you could describe your own blood-boiling, anger-inducing scenario from real life. It's only natural you would feel upset and angry. No one could blame you. But now, the question becomes this: What are you going to do with those red-hot emotions? How do you heed the words of Peter, "Be self-controlled...be compassionate and humble...Do not repay evil with evil or insult with insult, but with blessing, because to this you were called so that you may inherit a blessing"?[1]

Nine Anger Alleviators

What follows are nine strategies, each starting with the letter *A* for easy recall.

1. Acknowledge Your Anger

The first thing to do is *recognize* and *admit* to yourself when your internal temperature is rising. Become aware of your feelings of anger, and be alert to the temptation to suppress your emotions because of fear. It takes only a moment to stop and ask, "Okay, what's *really* going on inside of me?"

Be willing to take responsibility for any inappropriate anger. As Proverbs 28:13 states, "He who conceals his sins does not prosper, but whoever confesses and renounces them finds mercy."

If you find yourself getting mad, just admit it. Once you identify your feelings, you can deal with them. But if you deny or suppress them, they're bound to leak out—or explode—in unhealthy ways.

2. Assess the Source

We've talked about the four reasons we get angry: hurt, injustice, fear, and frustration. So when you start to get angry, it's helpful to identify what exactly is stirring up your emotions. Identify where your anger comes from:

- *hurt* feelings from the words or actions of others
- *unjust* actions of someone toward you or another person
- *fear* of some kind of loss
- *frustration* because something didn't go as you planned

Knowing precisely what is causing your flared-up feelings will enable you to respond wisely. If you know *what* you're dealing with, you'll know better *how* to deal with it. The Bible says, "Surely you desire truth in the inner parts; you teach me wisdom in the inmost place" (Psalm 51:6).

3. Analyze Your Temperament

Ask yourself the following questions:

- How often do I feel angry? (Always? Sometimes? Seldom?)
- How do I know when I am angry?
- How do others know when I am angry?
- How do I release my anger?

Do you explode? Do you become teary-eyed? Do you become sarcastic? Do you criticize? Do you become defensive?

As you seek to understand your style, pray...

"Test me, O Lord, and try me, examine my heart and my mind."[2]

4. Appraise Your Thinking

Those who call me on *Hope In The Night* almost always are experiencing some sort of problem or pain. I don't often encounter, nor do I expect, levity or humor from people pouring out their hearts to me late at night. So I was surprised by the fun call from Terri. But even lighthearted banter couldn't disguise her out-of-control thought life.

Terri: "I want you to tell me exactly what is wrong with me."

June: "Uh-oh! What's the matter?"

Terri: "I used to have a bad temper. I decided I needed either a shrink or a church...so I tried church. I trusted Jesus, but my temper didn't go away...it just went underground. Now I get mad in my mind. But there's an upside: I have a great time visualizing the things I want to do to people."

June: "Ahhh...like what? May I have an example?"

Terri: (laughing) "Well, the other day—right in front of my employees— my manager snatched a folder out of my hands. She just turned on her heel and walked away. Ever since then, in my mind, she's been suspended—head-first—outside my office window...which happens to be on the fifth floor of a downtown bank."

June: (laughing) "So you're telling me I should be grateful I have managed, so far, to stay on your good side!"

Terri: "Exactly! There was a time in my life when I didn't know these thoughts were wrong. But since giving my life to Christ, I know they are."

June: "Terri, I'm hearing you say, now that you're a Christian, you don't act out on your anger as you used to—you don't blow your top—but you're finding yourself struggling with your thought life. What's good is that you have a grasp of the danger of letting your thoughts go uncontrollably wild. Tell me, are you familiar with the concept of a spiritual stronghold?"

Terri: "It's an area of our lives that we can't seem to get the victory over. That's what this feels like to me."

June: "That's right. Strong emotions can distort your thinking. When your mind is under siege, it's helpful to intentionally pause and recognize what is going through your head. Paul tells us, 'Take captive every thought to make it obedient.'[3] We can grab hold of our thoughts to assess if they're accurate and truthful and if they pass the test of Philippians 4:8—true, noble, right, pure, lovely, admirable, excellent, and praiseworthy. This is the litmus test for taking our thoughts captive and making them obedient to Christ. If a thought flunks the test, it's to be thrown out—rejected and ejected from your mind."

As our call progressed, Terri and I talked about other ways to guard our minds from out-of-control anger. I explained that too often our anger is fueled by our own misinterpretations or misconceptions. When offended by someone, we can easily:

- *Exaggerate* the situation: "He said my presentation could be more polished. What he really means is that I *bombed*."
- *Assume* the worst: "She didn't show up for the party even though she promised to. *I think she probably hates me.*"
- *Mislabel* someone based on misconstrued actions: "I don't care if she insists she just 'misunderstood' or 'got her facts wrong'—*she's nothing but a liar*."
- Generalize: "He is *always* rude. He *never* says anything positive."

As we talked more, Terri began to grasp the importance of guarding her thought life in order to control her anger.

June: "Terri, our thoughts are filtered through our fears, our personal interpretations, and our past experiences. We would be wise to ask God to help us, because 'the Lord searches every heart and understands every motive behind the thoughts.'"[4]

Terri: "I'm beginning to understand. I need to look into my own heart, examine the issues that are making me angry, and ask God to help me see truth. If I can learn to evaluate my thinking accurately—compare it to what God says is true—my life will change...and so will my anger problem."

June: "Exactly!"

Terri seemed well on her way to getting her thought life under control—and with it, her runaway anger.

Now back to our nine anger alleviators.

5. Admit Your Needs

God creates each of us with three basic emotional needs—love, significance, and security—and there is nothing wrong with seeking to fulfill these needs.[5] The trouble comes when we inappropriately express anger as a means to getting these inner needs met.

Do you use anger as a manipulative ploy, demanding certain "musts" in an attempt to *feel loved*? Do you use anger as a tool for intimidation, always posturing to get your way in an attempt to *feel significant*? Do you use anger as a grasp for control, insisting on certain conditions in order to *feel secure*?

Ultimately, only Christ can meet all our inner needs for love, significance, and security. As Paul assures us, "My God will meet all your needs according to his glorious riches in Christ Jesus."[6]

6. Abandon Your Demands

Instead of demanding that others meet our inner need for *love*, we must allow the Lord to meet that need. We can pray, "Lord, though I would like to feel more love from others, I know You love me unconditionally." Listen to His response: "I have loved you with an everlasting love; I have drawn you with loving-kindness" (Jeremiah 31:3).

When it comes to our need for *significance*, we can pray, "Lord, though I would like to feel more significant to those around me, I know I am significant in Your eyes." Indeed, you are already significant to Him. He says, "I know the plans I have for you...plans to prosper you and not to harm you, plans to give you hope and a future" (Jeremiah 29:11).

And concerning our need for *security*, we can pray, "Lord, though I wish I felt more secure in my relationships, I know I am secure in my relationship with You." Be assured—God promises to meet that need. He says, "The LORD himself goes before you and will be with you; he will never leave you nor forsake you. Do not be afraid; do not be discouraged" (Deuteronomy 31:8).

Listen to the psalmist's reassurance: "The LORD is with me; I will not be afraid. What can man do to me?"[7]

It's true that God often uses people and circumstances to meet our needs, but when a critical need arises, we should choose to look first to our ultimate source of fulfillment, the Lord Himself.

7. Alter Your Attitudes

It's likely the process of introspection—looking deep within—will bring to light the need for some attitude adjustments. No surprise there. Anger has a way of turning positive thoughts into negative ones and generous intentions into selfish ones. Our goal is always to be more like Christ, putting others first, looking out for the interests of others, and not pushing our own rights.

Our minds produce a steady stream of thoughts, observations, and perceptions. These combine to shape the attitudes we have toward people and situations. When we're in a tense situation, the stream of thoughts speeds up and can become like a raging river. Suppose you could reach down into that current and pull out a thought. What would it be?

- *I am so mad! That guy is going to pay big time!*
- *She drives me crazy. I'm crossing her name off the list!*
- *What a jerk! How could he say such a thing?*
- *Who does she think she is? I'm going to put her in her place!*

If your flow of thoughts is headed in a negative direction, the outcome of your conflict will be negative as well. Conversely, if your stream is stocked with mostly positive thoughts, the outcome will probably be positive.

The Bible says, "Do nothing out of selfish ambition or vain conceit, but in humility consider others better than yourselves. Each of you should look not only to your own interests, but also to the interests of others."[8]

Through our own willpower and determination, we'll get only so far. We may be able to stamp out a few small grass fires here and there, but a raging inferno always threatens. Nevertheless, it is only through the power of God that we can achieve real, lasting change, which leads to our next point.

8. Access the Spirit's Power

It's amazing, and unfortunate, how often we fail to dip our ladle into the well of God's wisdom when we are thirsting for answers. Angry situations can confuse us and prompt us to make unwise choices. In reality, a bowl full of anger can quickly become a cauldron of chaos.

To prevent us from falling into a pattern of ungodly reactions, we need guidance that comes from heaven. Jesus gave us this promise: "When he, the Spirit of truth, comes, he will guide you into all truth."[9] Scripture tells us this kind of guidance is available to all believers who truly seek it.

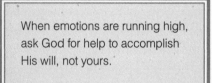

When emotions are running high, ask God for help to accomplish His will, not yours.

It may strike some as unrealistic to pause and pray right in the middle of an emotion-filled episode. But I submit to you this is precisely the time to seek God's wisdom, power, and the "peace...which transcends all understanding."[10] There is no need for a long, drawn-out prayer—a quick SOS sent heavenward is all that's needed to invite the Spirit of God to take control of your temper and tame your tongue.

The Lord knows what is in your heart. He knows if you desire to be humble and gracious in the most trying of times, and He will provide strength to carry you through—the ability to "let cooler heads prevail." God can use your anger to produce honorable results—correcting injustice, revealing deceit, or protecting victims. When emotions are running high, ask God for help to accomplish His will, not yours.

9. Address Your Anger to Bring About Positive Change

Now comes the tricky part: acting on all the information you've gathered. This is the moment when you ask, What am I going to do about it? What's the best response?

- *Determine* whether your anger is really justified. "A wicked man puts up a bold front, but an upright man gives thought to his ways."[11]

- *Decide* on the appropriate response. As Solomon tells us, "There is...a time to be silent and a time to speak."[12] How important is the issue? Would a good purpose be served if you mention it? Should you acknowledge your anger only to the Lord, or should you express it to the person involved?

- *Depend* on the Holy Spirit for guidance. Pour out your heart to God and seek His wisdom. Be sure to search the Scriptures for insight and take time to patiently wait upon the Lord (John 16:13).

- *Develop* constructive dialogue when you confront. Paul wrote, "Let your conversation be always full of grace, seasoned with salt, so that you may know how to answer everyone."[13] Keep these guidelines in mind:

  —*Don't* speak from a heart of unforgiveness.

  —*Do* think before you speak.

  —*Don't* use phrases such as "How could you?" or "Why can't you?"

  —*Do* use personal statements such as "I feel..."

  —*Don't* bring up past grievances.

  —*Do* stay focused on the present issue.

  —*Don't* assume the other person is wrong.

  —*Do* listen for feedback from another point of view.

- *Demonstrate* the grace of God by saying to yourself, *I placed my anger on the cross with Christ. I am no longer controlled by anger; I am alive with Christ living inside me.* As the apostle Paul said, "I have been crucified with Christ and I no longer live, but Christ lives in me. The life I live in the body, I live by faith in the Son of God, who loved me and gave himself for me" (Galatians 2:20).

And when I live this way, then...

- I will let Christ forgive through me.
- I will let Christ speak through me.
- I will let Christ love through me.

꿏

Putting the A's into Action

The next time you find yourself feeling the heat, take a moment to work through the list of anger alleviators. Doing so can save you from acting in ways you might regret later and spare yourself and others around you much heartache. The A-list serves as a guide to navigate through fiery scenarios with emotional and spiritual maturity. The more you utilize it, the more you'll be able to extinguish the most powerful blazes.

Creative Combustion

How to Fight for Right with Justifiable Anger

"'In your anger do not sin':
Do not let the sun go down while you are still angry"
(Ephesians 4:26).

CONSIDER: WHAT IS the difference between a rocket capable of carrying astronauts to the moon and a lethal bomb that can lay waste to whole cities? Both are loaded with dangerous and volatile fuel. Both explode with violent force. Both can serve humanity, and both can be used to commit crimes against humanity. What sets them apart?

Conclusion: *the intentions of the people who use them.*

Anger is a lot like rockets and bombs: It can be evil and dangerous, or it can be tremendously useful. Not everything that is ignited is destructive and deplorable. Sometimes a spark and a flame are exactly what we need to address critical issues or to get important work done.

It's true that intense heat can hurt people, but under the right conditions it can also become the catalyst for constructive transformation. I'm sure you would agree pancake batter isn't particularly appetizing until it's been on a sizzling hot griddle. And what good is a 5000-pound car without an internal combustion engine to release the explosive potential of gasoline and propel it down the road? The same is also true of fiery anger: It can spark a significantly sized flame for positive change.

Contrary to what we may have been taught, anger is not always an emotional dead end with no way out and no hope for change. It is more like a fork in the road. The destination you reach is up to you. Turn one direction—the way most commonly taken—and you enter a roadway where the final destination is destruction. This road leads only to pain, broken relationships, unforgiveness, and words and actions you will come to regret.

Channeling Anger into Positive Change

But like every fork in the road, there is an alternate path. To choose it, you must change your deeply ingrained thinking about anger. The misguided philosophy you learn from the world fits neatly on a bumper sticker: Don't get mad, get even!

On the road less traveled, however, you will learn a new way: to neither run from your anger nor give in to it, but to face it and direct its explosive power toward a beneficial purpose—the purpose God intends.

Every step you take in that direction harmonizes your life with the will of God. As Paul wrote, "Do not be conformed to this world, but be transformed by the renewal of your mind, that by testing you may discern what is the will of God, what is good and acceptable and perfect."[1]

And what begins as a personal commitment to transform your thinking and harness your anger might actually end up being used by God to bless countless lives. That's His specialty, you know—taking one person's commitment to transformation and causing it to spread like wildfire throughout a family, a community, a city, a country...and sometimes even the world.

The Scenario That Ignited Anger[2]

As a young man, César Chávez had more reason than most people to be angry. He already knew a lot about racial prejudice, social and economic injustice, and the personal pain they can cause. What he knew wasn't learned from books in history class at school; he lived it and experienced it every day.

César was born in 1927 on his family's small farm near Yuma, Arizona. In addition to working the land, his father, Librado, ran a local grocery store that did enough business for the family to get by. They were poor by modern standards, yet they didn't think of themselves that way.

César's mother, Juana, a devout Christian, was known for sharing what little they had with vagrants and others down on their luck. From her, César learned the importance of giving, and he developed an ironclad commitment to Christlike nonviolence that would define him later in life.

But the boy's world was far from perfect. He had been born into a society that considered people with his skin color and heritage to be inferior. Many in the community thought nothing of creating rules that made it more difficult for people like the Chávez family to prosper, even in the best of times. But the 1930s were not the best of times for anyone in America.

Through the early years of the Great Depression, Librado and Juana managed to stay on their land and feed their children. The kids spent half the day in school and the remaining hours working, either in the family store or in the fields.

However, by 1938, the economic stress became too much to handle and the Chávez family could no longer afford to pay property taxes on their farm. They were eligible for an emergency loan from the federal government, but the application was blocked numerous times by an unscrupulous local banker who wanted to buy the land himself for pennies on the dollar.

When the Chávez homestead was auctioned later that year, the only bidder was the bullying banker. César and his brother watched as he took possession of their home and tore down many of the structures their father had built.

This was just one event in a long history of unfair treatment at the hands of prejudiced neighbors and community leaders. And it burned in César's heart like a sweeping brush fire, spreading flames of indignation. For years, he and his family moved from place to place in California, picking crops in a harsh new life of never-ending, backbreaking labor.

Firsthand, César witnessed the deplorable conditions and unfair—even brutal—treatment the workers endured. He quit school after eighth grade. In 1944, he lied about his age and joined the Navy at 17, serving two years.

Yet even wearing a serviceman's uniform was not enough to break down the cultural barriers of segregation and discrimination when he returned home. He remembers a humiliating incident in a local diner:

> There was a sign on the door that said "white trade only" but we went in anyway. We heard they had these big hamburgers and we wanted one. There was a blonde, blue-eyed girl behind the counter. She said, "We don't serve Mexicans," and she laughed when she said it. She enjoyed doing that, laughing at us. We went out but I was real mad. Enraged. It had to do with my manhood.[3]

Who can blame him? Wouldn't you be angry if you'd been treated so disrespectfully? Especially after years of watching the people you cared for being cheated, oppressed, exploited, and exposed to dangerous and degrading working conditions? It is the kind of anger that has sparked raucous riots and even bloody revolutions.

The Pitchfork for Positive Change

Soon César had a family of his own and was working the fields of California beside his father and mother to put food on the table. His anger still smoldered deep within his heart. He had arrived at a crossroad. Would he go down the path of hostility and destruction, or would he channel his anger down another path and let it work for good?

> With God's help, you truly can rule anger instead of letting anger rule you.

To the benefit of millions of people, César chose the latter. Until his death in 1993, César Chávez devoted himself to bringing dignity and prosperity to poor, powerless farm workers all over America.

César's tireless and courageous work as founder of the United Farm Workers eventually won for farm laborers wage increases, health benefits, improved working conditions, and the right to bring grievances to their employers. As César's biographer pointed out:

> He taught [the people] to demand not just a better life, but an altogether different society. Taking literally Jesus' words in the Sermon on the Mount that "the last shall be first," Chávez gathered the farm workers and made them a peaceful force for social change.[4]

César Chávez could have become just another violent, angry young man. He could have started a gang instead of a social movement. But he chose to channel his anger for positive change, rather than allowing it to have a negative stronghold on his life.

Ways to Harness Your Heat

That same choice presents itself every time any of us gets angry. The issues at stake needn't be world-changing for your anger to become a positive force in your life. Sometimes the benefit can be as simple as an infusion of courage as you stand up to someone who mistreats you—a boss who unfairly takes credit for your work, a teenager who repeatedly shows disrespect for you and your rules, or a neighbor who spreads false rumors about your friend.

In any situation, no matter how seemingly small and mundane or massive and monumental, you are the one who decides what to do with your anger. Inward transformation resulting in outward change is always possible. With God's help, you truly can rule anger instead of letting anger rule you.

The challenge is making the right choice when your anger is at its peak boiling point. It takes both discipline and determination to refrain from lashing out and, instead, redirecting your "creative combustion" down a positive path. Here are four strategies to help you do just that:

Identify Your Objective

As we've already discussed, most of the time the purpose of your anger is pretty straightforward. You get angry as a way to...

- alleviate your *hurt*
- express outrage at an *injustice*
- confront your *fear*
- vent your *frustration*

And your goal in each case is simple: *Make it stop.*

But in order to redirect the explosive energy of your anger into a constructive pursuit, you've got to move beyond protective reflexes and ask yourself, *What do I want to accomplish? If my anger is a rocket I can steer, where do I want it to go?*

Answering those questions is a lot like creating a personal mission statement. Businesses and other organizations often put their philosophy and purpose in writing at their inception to let clients and the community know what to expect from them. This written document also becomes a navigational beacon for keeping purposes and goals on track. Being intentional about recording their objectives makes it easier for them to notice if they have wandered off course.

For the same reasons, when your mission is to make positive use of your anger, you will find it helpful to clearly state your intentions.

A Meddling Mother-in-Law

When Anita called me on *Hope In The Night*, she began by saying, "I know this will sound cliché, but my mother-in-law is driving me completely insane."

I assured her clichés exist for a reason. Just because an experience is common doesn't make it less real or painful.

For the first few years of their marriage, Tom and Anita lived hundreds of miles from either of their parents. At times, they regretted the limited contact the kids had with their grandparents. But on the whole, Tom and Anita were grateful for the freedom to establish their household as they saw fit.

All that changed when Tom's father died suddenly and his mother, Patricia, came to live nearby.

"She was in mourning—we all were—so for the first few months I let things slide that otherwise would have made me mad," Anita told me. "Now I'm just mad all the time, but after two years, it's hard to know what to do about it."

The problem was Patricia took on more responsibility and authority with her grandchildren than Anita wanted to relinquish. Patricia elbowed her way into Anita's parenting territory. She frequently reversed decisions her daughter-in-law made about important issues such as bedtime and how many treats the kids could have during the day.

Tom backed up Anita as best he could, but his job required him to travel and he was often unavailable. *Meddling* was the word most often written on the slips of paper blanketing the bottom of Anita's anger bowl.

"I've reached a breaking point," Anita said. "If I don't figure out how to get rid of my anger, it could get really ugly."

"It could get even uglier if you try to force your anger to just go away," I said. "That never works. How about this: If you could make your anger work toward a positive outcome, what would it be?"

She thought for a moment, then laughed as she said, "I was going to say I'd like Patricia to leave town again and never come back! But I realize that's not true. What I really want is to be treated with respect in my own home."

Bull's-eye! Although the way forward might still involve painful and even angry confrontation, the goal Anita identified was a worthy one. By targeting her anger on creating respect, Anita set a course that made it possible for everyone to win.

By stating her objective aloud, her blurred perception about what to do came into sharper focus. Don't let the destination of your anger remain vague or undefined. Set yourself a course for constructive resolution.

We can deceive ourselves by creating a smoke screen that makes us feel like we can change others. But we don't have the ability to change others. In fact, we don't even have the ability to truly change ourselves through our own will, strength, or desire. Change comes through our dependence on God's grace to transform lives—both ours and others.

This dependence on God is extremely important. For example, what if Anita's goal had been to force her mother-in-law to show her more respect? Her chances of success would have been next to zero. Why? It wasn't within Anita's power to make Patricia do things differently. Attempting to bring change in our own power generally results in the opposite of what we intend.

Resist or Respect

"Most of the time, the harder you push someone in a direction they don't want to go, the more they resist," I told Anita. "It is human nature. The best you can do is to make sure you respect yourself enough to draw firm boundaries and to enforce them, no matter who tries to step across the line."

At the time, that person was Patricia. The next time, it could be a neighbor or a church leader. If Anita did the work to alter her own inner landscape, she would be empowered and prepared to prevent another encroachment, whatever its source.

When you identify a positive goal for your anger, make sure it is achievable by concentrating on the only thing you can control: you.

Employ the Power of Prayer

After years of counseling hurting people on *Hope In The Night*, I am still surprised at how many attempt to struggle through life's hardships without taking advantage of one of God's greatest gifts: the privilege of prayer. Prayer is like making an SOS call to the Creator and Master of all things—yet this vital communication link and source of divine power too often goes unused. The Bible says, "You do not have, because you do not ask" (James 4:2). It's like we're trying to control our anger with our hearts and minds disconnected from their power source. And it's both frustrating and futile, for the result is certain failure.

Unfortunately, too many people perceive prayer more as a dreary duty than a precious privilege. To pray is not to beg or to engage in wishful thinking. It is to stand before God as sons and daughters in the full confidence of our salvation and to trust Him to answer our prayers according to His perfect will.

> True empathy, tapped by prayer, will open pathways to peace you hadn't seen before or believed possible.

God's eagerness to answer prayer is reflected in the words of the apostle John: "This is the confidence we have in approaching God: that if we ask anything according to his will, he hears us. And if we know that he hears us—whatever we ask—we know that we have what we asked of him" (1 John 5:14-15).

If you struggle with anger and want to make a commitment to channel your churning into a positive force, there is no better way to start than by having a candid conversation with God.

First, pray for discernment. As theologian Reinhold Niebuhr wrote in his famous *Serenity Prayer:* "God grant me the serenity to accept the things I cannot change, the courage to change the things I can, and the wisdom to know the difference." When our hearts and minds are open to His leading, the Spirit will guide us into all truth.

Second, pray for those with whom you are in conflict. Ask God to give you insight and understanding into why they think and behave as they do. You will certainly discover your "enemies" are only human—misguided, perhaps—but just as vulnerable to pain and fear as you are.

True empathy, tapped by prayer, will open pathways to peace you hadn't seen before or even believed possible.

Finally, pray for God's will, not yours, to be done. We've all prayed for things and later thanked God for not answering our prayers with a *yes*. And we've all heard accounts of people attending high school reunions, seeing their former sweethearts, and thanking God for not answering the prayers voiced by their foolish young hearts years before.

The truth is, the human eye is not well adapted to see the big picture. We have trouble perceiving the value of paradox and mystery. When it comes to harnessing anger for good, what looks like a setback is sometimes the key to victory. It is important to surrender to God's purpose no matter what.

As Proverbs 3:5-6 says, "Trust in the LORD with all your heart and lean not on your own understanding; in all your ways acknowledge him, and he will make your paths straight." That's good advice. To "acknowledge him" refers to seeking God in prayer, seeking His perfect will in all situations, including dealing with your battle with blazing anger. God *wants* to be involved; He is eager to help and strengthen you.

How do you release your anger through prayer? First, delve deeply into your heart and honestly reflect on the pain you are holding on to. Then go to God in all humility, refusing to demand your rights and rejecting any thought of revenge, and surrender the situation and yourself—past, present, and future—to the Lord. Although you, like Anita, may feel completely powerless, in reality you have the power to release your pain and anger to Him and thereby engage His all-powerful involvement in your situation.

The "Releasing Your Anger" Prayer

"Lord Jesus, thank You for loving me;
thank You for caring about me.
Because You know everything,
You know the strong sense of (￼ hurt, injustice, fear, frustration)
I have felt about (name or situation).
Thank You for understanding my anger.
Right now, I release all my anger to You.
I trust You with my future and with me.
In Christ's name I pray. Amen."

Tangible Action: Using Anger for Good

What good would it have done for César Chávez or Martin Luther King Jr. or William Wilberforce (the English abolitionist who fought against slavery) to channel their anger at injustice into positive change if they had never set foot out of their houses? Not much, I'd say. Only because they stepped into society and turned angry passion into viable action do millions of us enjoy a more egalitarian world.

The same is required of you if you hope to translate your anger into positive change, if you hope to turn wishful thinking into progress you can measure. Once you know what you want to accomplish, decide what you must *do* to make it happen...and then do it.

For Anita that meant finally sharing her feelings with her mother-in-law, a conversation she had avoided for years. She kept her goal in mind as she planned how and when to broach the subject, making sure the two of them would not be interrupted. She carefully scripted her initial comments to avoid making inflammatory accusations.

"I realized I could succeed in reaching my goal no matter how Patricia reacted," Anita told me later. "Once I defined my boundaries, she was free to honor them, or not. And I was free to continue accepting old patterns of behavior, or not.

"It was so liberating! Why should I stuff my anger down and watch it turn to bitterness when I could draw strength from it instead?"

The key to Anita's "liberation" was respecting herself enough to establish firm boundaries and enforce them, plus a willingness to act on her anger positively so she could reach her goal. At first, Patricia reacted as Anita feared she might. She was defensive and resistant. But Anita was undeterred, like Chávez and his farm workers on a picket line. Eventually Anita's firm yet gentle determination paid off as Patricia admitted to being too intrusive, and apologized.

"It was like the relationship was reborn," Anita said. "From that time on, she treated me more as an equal. She even confided for the first time how much she still grieved for her husband, and I was able to help her through it. None of that would have happened if I hadn't trusted my anger and used it to set things right."

As Anita surrendered her bowl of anger to God, He melted each "meddling" slip—forever.

※

Anger can be frightening. It can thunder and roar. It can erupt and blow, and bury your life in smoldering ash. But if you'll resist the temptation to run from your anger—if you'll heed it and harness its energy for good—like the engine of a Boeing 747, it can deliver the thrust you need to rise above hurt, injustice, fear, and frustration. And it can help you soar to new heights—enough to even possibly change the world!

Bomb Squad Basics
How to Handle Hotheaded People

*"Do not make friends with a hot-tempered man,
do not associate with one easily angered"*
(Proverbs 22:24).

I'M NOT A very good person," Sylvia declared when I prompted her to share why she had called me on *Hope In The Night*. Most people who phone in—especially those in great pain—have a determined, demonstrative quality to their voice. They are calling because they've finally had enough of some difficult circumstance they are facing. I listen for this last-hope resignation in their voice because it's evidence of a readiness to let God intervene in their circumstances and lead them toward emotional and spiritual healing and health.

I'm *Supposed* to Take It

Sylvia sounded lifeless, flat, and utterly defeated. Her voice had the telltale emptiness of someone who has given up on herself. Later I learned it wasn't Sylvia's idea to phone in. A concerned friend dialed the studio number and put the phone in Sylvia's hand.

"What makes you think that about yourself?" I gently asked when she referred to herself as a substandard person.

After a lengthy pause, she said, "My husband, Gene, has a terrible temper. I don't blame him for that. He came from a very angry family, so it's pretty much all he knows. I've tried to love him unconditionally, to lay down my life and turn the other cheek—all those things God expects me to do. But I always fail miserably, and things just get worse."

At that point, I suspected Sylvia's ideas about how to handle an angry person—and what it takes to be a good wife—were significantly different from God's. Something had indeed gone wrong in her life, but probably not in the way she imagined. I asked her to describe her relationship with Gene. What did she mean when she said that, despite her efforts, things "get worse"?

"I always know I've pushed him too far when he gets in a rage and starts swearing uncontrollably or throwing things," she said.

"That sounds extreme," I told her.

"Well, he doesn't throw things *at me*," she explained. "He's not really abusive, just angry. Usually he gets that way after I've become angry myself."

Right away it seemed to me Sylvia excused her husband's rage because she thought that's what God expects of her, as if it was His will for her to suffocate beneath Gene's pile of paper slips in his colossal anger bowl. And she blamed herself for provoking him, as if she was the detonator for his explosive temper.

As a result, Sylvia couldn't see Gene's unresolved anger as abusive. Most of us would readily identify throwing things, slamming doors, and yelling without restraint as abusive behavior. Its presence day after day creates a climate of fear that is severely damaging to any relationship.

Although Gene's anger could apparently be ignited by any number of things Sylvia said or did, the most incendiary issue in their relationship was money. He kept tight control over what she was allowed to spend, yet he would often bring home expensive electronic gadgets or power tools he seldom used. If Sylvia questioned a purchase, Gene would start shouting and defend his right to spend his hard-earned money as he pleased. She also suspected he gambled a good deal with his coworkers and on occasion lost considerable amounts of money.

"I used to believe if I could just love him well enough, he'd see there was no need to be so angry at me or the world," Sylvia said. "Now I think it must be God's will for me to just love him unconditionally in spite of how he treats me. The only problem is, I just can't seem to do it…not for long, anyway." Again, there was defeat and heartbreaking heaviness in her voice.

"I certainly agree with that last part," I said. "You *can't* do it."

There was silence as she thought about that.

> God sets clear limits on what behavior He will accept.

"You can't do it because you shouldn't do it," I continued.

"I shouldn't love my husband?" she asked, as if she hadn't heard me correctly.

"No—what I mean is, you shouldn't assume it's ever God's perfect will for you to suffer abusive mistreatment from anyone for any reason, and especially not from your husband," I replied.

Misconceptions About Turning the Other Cheek

Over the years, I've learned how startling that statement can be to many people—both men and women. Somewhere along the way, we have mistaken God's exhortation to love our enemies and to turn the other cheek as commandments to become doormats in His name.

Even though God sets clear limits on what behaviors He will accept, we somehow believe He has prohibited us from doing the same for ourselves. We allow abuse on the false assumption that holding an offender accountable is less godly than quietly accepting the mistreatment and hoping the person will eventually see God's love in it. Surely the Lord wants better for His children.

When it comes to dealing with angry people, this flaw in our thinking is the first and most formidable obstacle we have to overcome. In truth, offering no resistance to angry people can actually work *against* helping them resolve the issues that make them angry in the first place.

In Sylvia's case, what incentive did Gene have for confronting his own pain and subsequent anger when he was free to dish out abusive behavior day after day with no repercussions and no consequences? Indeed, God's will for Sylvia was to require dignity and respect in *all* of her relationships, including her marriage with Gene.

Self-Defense or Going on the Offensive

It is true there is often a fine line between self-defense and going on the offensive. You cross that line the moment you set out to cause reciprocal pain toward someone who has wounded you, rather than simply preventing further harm to yourself. That's a trap Christians are right to painstakingly avoid. As the apostle Paul wrote, "Do not grieve the Holy Spirit of God, with whom you were sealed for the day of redemption. Get rid of all bitterness, rage and anger, brawling and slander, along with every form of malice."[1]

But many people operate on the other end of the spectrum, avoiding conflict at all costs. In the name of what they mistakenly think is Christlike love, they don't set healthy boundaries for themselves.

There is a big difference between the "brawling and slander" and "malice" Paul warned us about, and justifiable self-preservation. Misunderstanding this distinction renders us powerless to protect ourselves from mistreatment and abuse—primarily because of this one reason: *We don't believe we even have a right to defend ourselves.*

Private Property, No Trespassing

Look around. Society is full of signs sending messages about personal rights and the boundaries that protect them, such as "Private property. Keep out." We know to cross those boundaries by invitation only—or face the consequences of violating another's right to protect their property. Our legal system provides backup, making it a punishable crime to trespass and to steal, destroy, or vandalize someone else's possessions. These judicial laws help form the foundation of civilized society.

All abusive husbands—Christian or not—seem to know this one scripture: "Wives, submit to your husbands."[2] The all-too-prevalent mind-set is that a wife must submit to all mistreatment at the hands of her husband. There is no recourse, for that is God's will.

However, anyone who decidedly wants to be in God's will *must* know what God says in His Word in the context of the *whole* Bible. We must correct the confusion that is degrading wives worldwide.

Correcting the Confusion

The woman who sincerely wants to please God but is not grounded in the Word of God can become captive to an incorrect understanding of biblical submission. All too easily she will *accept* abuse, thinking it is right when God says it is wrong.

Likewise, the man who sincerely wants to please God but who is not grounded in the Word of God can become captive to an incorrect understanding of sacrificial love. All too easily he will *accept* abuse, thinking it is right when God says it is wrong. One key to correcting the confusion is to read Scripture passages in light of their context. So when we read, "Wives, submit to your husbands" or "Husbands, love your wives, just as Christ loved the church," we need to…

- look at the surrounding verses.
- look at the purpose of the passage or book in which the verse is found.
- look at the whole counsel of God's Word on submission and love and how we are to relate to one another: "Do your best to present yourself to God as one approved, a workman who does not need to be ashamed and who correctly handles the word of truth" (2 Timothy 2:15).

When I was teaching in Russia, Ukraine, and Romania, I remember the sincere attitudes of many pastors and spiritual leaders who assumed that wives had to submit to abuse. I said, "Show me the scriptures you are using to substantiate this position"—and indeed they did. The next day I addressed each one of their scriptural misconceptions. At the conclusion they said, "We've never heard teaching on this. We've known that somehow violence was wrong, but never knew what to say."

I want to give you this assurance: You are going to be the knight in shining armor—the desperately needed "Good Samaritan"—when you know how to help a woman suffering the devastating pain and the demoralizing shame of domestic violence. (The statistics are one out of every three women *worldwide*.)

Here are the arguments and answers regarding this matter:

Argument: When Jesus said, "Turn the other cheek," He meant that marriage partners should submit to abuse.[3]

Answer: When you look at the words of Jesus, the context is the issue of retaliation: Refuse to retaliate evil for evil. Jesus was not saying we should willingly accept abuse.

> *"You have heard that it was said, 'Eye for eye, and tooth for tooth.'*
> *But I tell you, Do not resist an evil person. If someone strikes you*
> *on the right cheek, turn to him the other also"*
> (MATTHEW 5:38-39).

The backdrop of "turning the other cheek" was refusing to take personal revenge rather than promoting or accepting abuse.

Argument: Because Jesus submitted Himself to abuse, people who want to be Christlike must also submit to abuse.

Answer: It is important to notice that on numerous occasions when the enemies of Jesus sought to harm Him, He eluded them and escaped. However, when the time came for Him to take away the sins of the world, Jesus allowed His blood to be the payment to purchase our forgiveness. Clearly, Jesus did not submit to abuse, except when it was time for Him to go to the cross.

"Jesus went around in Galilee, purposely staying away from
Judea because the Jews there were waiting to take his life...
Again they tried to seize him, but he escaped their grasp"
(JOHN 7:1; 10:39).

Argument: In 1 Peter 2 we are called to endure "unjust suffering." Therefore, abused mates should consider such suffering as commendable before God.

"It is commendable if a man bears up under the pain
of unjust suffering because he is conscious of God"
(1 PETER 2:19).

Answer: The context of this passage in 1 Peter refers to suffering "because [you] are conscious of God," which means suffering ridicule, criticism, and rejection because of your faith, not because you are someone's mate.

God does not call anyone to accept abuse from their mates. To the contrary, spouses who abuse their mates do so because of their own ungodliness. In fact, God specifically calls husbands and wives to sacrificially love each other and treat each other with respect.

"Wives, in the same way be submissive to your husbands...
so that they may be won over without words by [your] behavior...
Husbands, in the same way be considerate as you live with your wives,
and treat them with respect as the weaker partner and as heirs with you of
the gracious gift of life, so that nothing will hinder your prayers"
(1 PETER 3:1,7).

Argument: An abused mate should view suffering as a legitimate "cross" to be taken up and carried for the sake of Christ.

"If anyone would come after me [Jesus],
he must deny himself and take up his cross and follow me"
(MATTHEW 16:24).

Answer: Nowhere does the Bible indicate that the cross is an instrument of physical and emotional pain to be inflicted upon a mate. In context, Jesus was saying that the cross is a symbol of death—death to self-centered living, death to self-rule so that the Lord can rule our hearts and lives. The very next verse confirms that the cross stands for yielding our lives to the Lord, not yielding our lives to abuse.

> *"Whoever wants to save his life will lose it,*
> *but whoever loses his life for me will find it"*
> (MATTHEW 16:25).

Argument: God made men superior to women.

Answer: God made women and men different from one another, with different roles and functions. The Bible does not say that God regards one gender as superior and the other as inferior; rather, He regards them as equal.

> *"There is neither Jew nor Greek, slave nor free,*
> *male nor female, for you are all one in Christ Jesus"*
> (GALATIANS 3:28).

Argument: Because Ephesians 5:21 says, "Submit to one another," a mate must submit unconditionally—even to abuse.[4]

Answer: This conclusion contradicts other scriptures. A hierarchy of submission is demonstrated when the apostles refuse to obey the high priest and instead obey the Great Commission by continuing to teach in the name of Jesus (Matthew 28:19-20). They committed a severely punishable offense by directly disobeying the high priest in order to submit to God.

Similarly, if a mate expects a marriage partner to do something that God says is wrong, the partner is to disobey the erring mate in order to submit to God. Our Lord clearly states His opposition to violence, as well as His position that spouses are to treat their mates with respect.

> *"Peter and the other apostles replied:*
> *'We must obey God rather than men!'"*
> (ACTS 5:29).

Argument: Because the Bible says, "The husband is the head of the wife," a wife must not resist being abused by her husband.[5]

Answer: A wife is to submit to the *headship* of her husband, but the Bible nowhere implies she is to submit to the abuse from her husband. She is to respect his position, not be victimized by his power.

In Ephesians 5:23, the husband-wife relationship is compared to the relationship between Christ and the church. Christ is "the head of the church, his body." Although the husband is the head of his wife, no head abuses its own body. A husband never chooses to beat his body—unless, of course, he is "out of his head" (mentally ill)! Instead, he does whatever he can to protect and provide for his own body. A godly man will treat his wife in the same way.

> *"The husband is the head of the wife as Christ is the head*
> *of the church, his body, of which he is the Savior...*
> *husbands ought to love their wives as their own bodies.*
> *He who loves his wife loves himself. After all, no one ever hated*
> *his own body, but he feeds and cares for it,*
> *just as Christ does the church"*
> (EPHESIANS 5:23,28-29).

How Could She Tell Anyone?

Intelligent, competent, assured—these words painted the picture of my friend Gail, an attractive, energetic young woman whom I had known casually for more than ten years. But when I received word that, at the hands of her husband, she had been a victim of repeated violence, my first thought was, *How could this be?*

After all, Gail had worked several years at a Christian ministry training people how to study the Bible. Then she attended a respected seminary, where she met her future husband, Andy. However, after they married, her confidence decreased and her fear increased. Unbeknownst to family and friends, Gail was being abused.

But how could she tell anyone? She wanted to protect the image of her little family. Surely if she "tried hard enough" he would stop and tenderly love her—that's what all abused women typically think.

> We have a heavenly Father who wants us to be safe and secure—physically, emotionally, and spiritually.

But not so. Now Andy was divorcing her for another woman, and they were in the midst of a custody battle over their two young sons. The judge ruled that until a decision was made as to which parent would have custodial care, this arrangement was to be followed: The children were to stay in the home, and each parent would rotate in and out every other week. So every other week for about a year and a half, Gail stayed in my home.

We had many late-night talks. The one that stands out most in my memory is the evening I asked if she had any pictures to prove to the judge that Andy was an untrustworthy, violent man. Immediately she went to the guest bedroom and returned with pictures of herself—police photographs—that showed her head severely bruised and swollen.

I was stunned. I hadn't expected such graphic pictures. (Andy had denied the abuse, claiming instead that she had inflicted the injuries on herself—a common "blame game" tactic!)

When I gave Gail our *Biblical Counseling Keys* on wife abuse, she quickly affirmed what the material said about many wife batterers being adept at manipulating their wives with scriptures such as, "Wives, submit to your husbands," yet they themselves are careless about heeding all the verses against violence. (And sadly, as of yet, I have never talked with a wife who has heard scriptures presented from the pulpit that encourage her to seek the protection she so desperately needs if she is being abused.) Rather, after an incident of wife abuse, too many women hear disheartening, foolish statements like, "What did you do to cause it?" as though the husband's violent sin is her fault. This, tragically, doubly victimizes the woman.

No wonder many women who suffer abuse are confused and distressed. They wonder, *Must I really suffer at the hands of someone who has sworn to protect and cherish me? And where is God when I am hurting so much?*

Not only is God with those who suffer, He also has provided a way of deliverance through His Word. The joy of victory and healing is available to any who seek it. My prayer is that the biblical truths shared within the pages of this book will be used by God to free you or someone you know from the shackles of unjust suffering.

> *"Then you will know the truth,*
> *and the truth will set you free"*
> (JOHN 8:32).

Now, for the rest of the story. First, after two years, my friend was awarded custody of her children. Second, the judge admitted that, in retrospect, his better judgment would have been to assign only one parent custodial care until a permanent decision was made. And last, tragically, Andy served no time in jail and received no sentence for his abuse.

We All Have God-Given Rights

Consider the following "bomb squad basics"—ground rules for relating to the angry people in your life:

1. You have the right to be safe from physical and emotional harm

It is staggering to realize how many people suffer needlessly at the hands of angry, abusive people because they think God is calling them to stick it out in unsafe situations. I've talked with far too many wounded women—women who are precious to God—who remained in abusive marriages in the name of submission. I've heard from employee after employee who endured crass conduct and cruel behavior from their bosses because they felt God wanted them to put up with such treatment. And I've spoken with countless people who, assuming it was God's will, remained in friendships in which they were continually used and manipulated.

Situations like these are complex, and there is no one-size-fits-all solution. But be assured of this: We have a heavenly Father who wants us to be safe and secure—physically, emotionally, and spiritually.

In most societies, a parent who deliberately puts a child in danger is scorned and punished. Yet some people mistakenly believe our heavenly Father puts us in perilous situations with no concern for our safety and leaves us to fend for ourselves. To the contrary, we have a God who is lovingly committed to our well-being. Jesus assured,

> *"Which of you, if his son asks for bread, will give him a stone? Or if he asks for a fish, will give him a snake? If you, then, though you are evil, know how to give good gifts to your children, how much more will your Father in heaven give good gifts to those who ask him!"*[6]

Here's the bottom-line truth: You have a right to be safe. God is never pleased or honored when His people are mistreated in abusive relationships. When He encouraged us to rejoice when we encounter various trials,[7] He was *not* saying pain and trauma are always part of His will for us. Rather, He was saying trials are inevitable in a sinful world filled with sinful people who do sinful things.

But the good news is these very trials can provide a valuable opportunity to grow and mature as Christians. And if we love God, He promises to use our every experience for our good. Living with an angry person has the challenging potential to teach us how to protect ourselves in firm, loving, godly ways and to stop ignoring our abuse by suffering in silence.

2. You have the right to set your own boundaries

Only you know what behavior hurts your heart or makes you feel threatened and uncomfortable. And only you can decide what behavior you will accept and what you won't. That right belongs to you alone. For example, because Gene grew up in a home where aggressive actions and attitudes among family members were commonplace, he often chided Sylvia for being oversensitive if she objected to his angry outbursts. Unconcealed hostility that Gene called "normal" made Sylvia feel frightened and insecure. Consider Gene's "justifications":

- "Come on! I was only joking!"
- "Everybody gets mad and flies off the handle sometimes. Don't make a federal case out of it."
- "Lighten up, will you?"
- "So what if I get mad? You're the one making a big deal out of it."

Comments like these are clues that the angry person wants to control you by having the final say in where your boundaries are drawn. As I told Sylvia, your boundaries are just that—*yours*. In fact, setting standards for yourself is more than a right. Proverbs 4:23 tells us it is an important responsibility: "Above all else, guard your heart, for it is the wellspring of life."

3. You have the right to enforce your boundaries with consequences for encroachment

Hopefully, you have claimed your right to be safe and to stay safe by setting boundaries. Wonderful! Your next step in successfully dealing with angry people is affirming your right to insist on repercussions when a boundary has been crossed and when trespassers refuse to retreat—even if they are spouses. They too must know there are consequences for angrily screaming, smashing, and slamming their way into your territory.

4. You have the right to defend your cause

Many believers fear being too quick to defend their borders and impose repercussions. In taking to heart Paul's admonition to live up to our calling as Christians "bearing with one another in love, eager to maintain the unity of the Spirit in the bond of peace,"[8] too often we wind up taking no action at all. Naturally, that communicates to those whose anger spews into our territory that our boundaries are not real, but only imaginary and not to be taken seriously.

However, the phrase "bearing with one another" in Ephesians 4:2 doesn't mean we are to ignore sinful behavior. Rather, it means we are to accept our differences.

Jesus affirmed our right, our obligation to impose consequences on someone who has wronged us:

> *"If your brother sins against you, go and show him his fault,*
> *just between the two of you. If he listens to you, you have won*
> *your brother over. But if he will not listen, take one or two others*
> *along, so that 'every matter may be established by the testimony*
> *of two or three witnesses.' If he refuses to listen to them,*
> *tell it to the church; and if he refuses to listen even to the church,*
> *treat him as you would a pagan or a tax collector"*
> (MATTHEW 18:15-17).

It's simple: If someone sins against you, your God-given right and responsibility is to confront—with a stinging rebuke, if necessary. If the person is clearly in the wrong but fails to take responsibility for the misbehavior, consequences must be enacted.

Three Keys to Peace (or at Least a Cease-Fire)

Now that you know God has empowered you with the right to live in safety and peace, you are ready to learn the art of "de-escalation" in any conflict with an angry person.

Fair warning: This isn't always easy. It requires a challenging blend of toughness and compassion, determination and patience, humility and self-respect. But the payoff is there for anyone willing to do the work. As an old German proverb says, "God makes the nuts, but He doesn't crack them."[9] You've got to do that part yourself. Here's how:

1. Don't Pour Gasoline on the Fire

If there is one thing that acts like gasoline doused on someone's fiery anger, it is *more* anger, coming from another source. Yes, you have the right to be safe, to set boundaries, and to stand firm when those boundaries are broken. But using fiery anger to retaliate against fiery anger is the path least likely to lead to peace and most likely will lead to war. In fact, it can just as easily change you from an innocent victim to a guilty anger accomplice.

> *"There is…a time to be silent and a time to speak"*
> (Ecclesiastes 3:1,7).

It is important to stay calm when dealing with an angry person. Remember, anger is an extremely powerful emotion that God's Spirit— who lives in you—can both tame and temper. It has no power in and of itself to force you to respond one way or another.

Anger is contagious only if we let it be. Above all, don't allow sparks from someone else's anger to ignite your own.

Proverbs 15:1 tells us, "A gentle answer turns away wrath, but a harsh word stirs up anger." If you habitually respond to anger with a "gentle answer," you'll see the other person's wrath diminish, *as well as your own.*

2. Don't Hesitate to Evacuate

If you were to suddenly become aware that you were holding a live grenade, I'm pretty sure what you would do—toss it or drop it, and run! Yet when it comes to dealing with an explosive person, many of us ignore the best defense: keep a safe distance. We remain engaged in battle, on the angry person's terms, long past when it is productive or prudent to do so. Perhaps it's because we feel withdrawal is the same as surrender. But every good general knows retreating and regrouping today is sometimes the only way to advance tomorrow.

Here's the bottom line: Protecting yourself is paramount. In extreme cases, where physical violence is an imminent possibility, it is vital you leave immediately. Don't wait until the first blow is struck. If you feel threatened, go! *Now.*

But even when you aren't subject to bodily harm, there is no need to submit to an angry emotional beating either. It is important to learn how to recognize when the heat of rage has burned away any possibility of reason or compromise. When that happens, it is time to retreat to avoid further emotional abuse. The "time-out" can last minutes, hours, days, or longer because self-protection is the priority.

The point is, you are entitled to maintain a safe distance as long as you continue to feel threatened by the flames of fury. The Bible tells us, "A prudent man sees danger and takes refuge, but the simple keep going and suffer for it" (22:3).

3. Call for Reinforcements

Sylvia's friend, the one who dialed the number the night Sylvia spoke to me on *Hope In The Night,* understood we are seldom called to face a giant one-on-one like David did Goliath. More often, we are empowered to face our angry enemies in the strength and safety of supportive company—friends, family members, fellow believers, a trusted pastor, or a professional counselor. When physical violence is present, help can also come in the form of court orders and police protection.

The truth is, an angry person's chief weapon against you is psychological and emotional control—something that's all too easy to achieve when you are isolated and alone. You need others to remind you of your rights and to stand with you in securing the boundaries you set for yourself.

Sylvia eventually saw the wisdom in that. With the help of a support group for abused women at her church, she began to change her mistaken beliefs about what God expected of her and claimed her right to be safe. As a result, she moved out of the house for a period of separation to let Gene know she was serious about being free from his angry, threatening behavior.

"I could never have done that without backup," she told me later. "Others helped me see it wasn't about changing Gene. Only God can do that, and I still pray He will. But now, it is about changing me and protecting myself and making the most of the life God gave *me*."

The biblical call and necessity of giving tangible support is undeniably clear:

> *"Rescue those being led away to death; hold back those*
> *staggering toward slaughter. If you say, 'But we knew nothing*
> *about this,' does not he who weighs the heart perceive it?*
> *Does not he who guards your life know it? Will he not repay*
> *each person according to what he has done?"*
> (PROVERBS 24:11-12).

Don't battle the blazing fires of anger alone. Even firefighters know not to send one of their own alone into a burning building. Engage reinforcements, and be better prepared to face anger flare-ups.

※

Out of Harm's Way

Your heavenly Father wants you to be safe and free from the effects of living with an angry person. But He never intends for you to take harmful risks in securing a safe and peaceful environment.

God expects you to love angry people, to forgive them, to treat them as you would wish to be treated—but at a safe distance. He does not expect you to helplessly endure and continue to facilitate their fiery incursions into your territory.

Know your rights.
Draw your boundaries.
Guard them firmly.

Quenching the Coals

How to Plan Ahead for Anger Flare-Ups

"The wise turn away wrath"
(PROVERBS 29:8 ESV).

EACH WEEKNIGHT, DURING our live two-hour call-in counseling program *Hope In The Night*, people call to share their life struggles and to receive real solutions. Regularly, I hear callers say things like:

"My temper comes out of nowhere—like a monster in my closet!"

"I live with a rage-aholic, and we all walk on eggshells."

"She makes me furious, but now my own anger frightens me!"

Many people feel miffed for even experiencing anger in the first place. They don't know where it comes from, and don't know what to do with it. What they do know is it causes pain, and they want to get rid of it.

Anger by Another Name

During the first year that our small Hope For The Heart staff in Dallas, Texas, met for a weekly devotional, I asked everyone around the circle to share what angers them the most. After I and several other team members had shared, I turned to the person to my right and asked, "What angers you the most?" Looking at me with the sweetest smile, Nancy batted her beautiful brown eyes and said, "I don't get angry."

"You don't ever get angry?" I probed. "No," she answered confidently. "Really?" I questioned. Again, she responded ever so sweetly, "No, really."

So we went on to the next person, who explained that her anger arose when, as a pastor's wife, she and her children had been criticized for not being "perfect." Then the next person said, "Well, I begin to feel angry when I want to communicate but I get no response. I get put off, then I feel rejected. That really hurts!"

We were more than halfway around the circle when Nancy—who has to be one of the dearest people in the world—interrupted: "June, excuse me. I just realized I *do* get angry. I really do; I just always called it *frustration*!" It turned out Nancy did have an anger bowl—she just identified it by another name.

Sadly, the sum total of what most of us think or know about anger is this: We have it, and we don't like it—not in ourselves, and certainly not in others. Anger is usually as welcome as a broken toe or a bad toothache.

Who can blame us? Anger can be dangerous, destructive, and dysfunctional. It can make us feel embarrassed and ashamed or wounded and victimized, depending on whether we're dishing it out or receiving it. We've all seen the devastating damage anger can do to relationships, physical and mental health, and spiritual well-being.

When we are drawn into anger-inducing situations, we need to not be at the mercy of our emotions. Impulsive, knee-jerk responses can result in deep regret. God gives us the power to be assertive without being aggressive, resolute without seeking revenge.

When you are angry, does reason rule or do tense emotions take charge? Do you allow the mind of Christ within you to determine how you should act, making a choice that leads to *appropriate action*, or do you give a hasty response that leads to an *inappropriate reaction*?

If you have never evaluated what happens when you feel angry, or if you lack insight as to how others perceive you when you are angry, seek God's wisdom and understanding. The writer of Proverbs tells us:

> "If you call out for insight and cry aloud for understanding,
> and if you look for it as for silver and search for it as for hidden treasure,
> then you will understand the fear of the LORD and find the

knowledge of God. For the LORD *gives wisdom, and from his mouth*
come knowledge and understanding"
(PROVERBS 2:3-6).

How can we learn to act (with conviction, clarity, and confidence)
rather than react (out of compulsion, confusion, and callousness)? The
first step is to simply recognize that knee-jerk reacting is not likely to
produce a helpful outcome. In fact, it will probably make matters worse.
Acting with a clear head and conscience, on the other hand, helps us
achieve positive, godly results. Consider Darren, a man quite trans-
parent about his anger and eager for transformation.

The Proverbs Project

On a Friday years ago, I traveled to Orlando, Florida, for a week
of speaking and media engagements. I felt blessed to stay in the home
of an exceptional couple, Darren and Diana, along with their teenage
daughter, Tina. I've never felt more warmly welcomed and included.

On Monday morning, I sat at the kitchen table with Diana, sharing how much I admired Darren.

"He's wonderful—a totally trustworthy husband," she said. Then
she confided, "But for as long as I've known him—26 years—he's had
an anger problem. It really concerns me."

I listened empathetically and nodded. Then Diana quickly moved
on to other topics.

On Tuesday afternoon, I chatted with Tina about her senior year,
her high school graduation, and her plans for college. Then the conversation came around to her parents. She shared how supportive they
were. But then she leaned in close and whispered, "I love my dad so
much. I just wish he didn't have such a bad temper."

I was surprised she brought this up—unprompted. I had not mentioned anything her mom had shared.

Then on Wednesday night, Darren said, "I know you've got a television appearance in West Palm Beach on Friday. I have some business
I could do in West Palm, if you'd like for me to drive you."

"That's wonderful!" I exclaimed.

So Friday morning, during our three-hour trek, Darren and I discussed his business, his heart for God, and bits and pieces about his background.

After a couple hours of conversation, he apparently felt comfortable enough to interject, "June, there's a problem I've struggled with for a long time. I've never figured out how to control my anger. No matter how hard I try, I just keep failing. Do you have any ideas?"

Impressed at his authenticity and humility, I offered, "Would you be willing to do a project for a month? Just read the thirty-one chapters of Proverbs, one chapter a day for a month. Begin with the first chapter, reading slowly so the words will sink into your mind and heart. Each day, write down any verses about anger or speech or attitude. When you're finished," I explained, "review the verses you've written and ask the Lord what He wants you to learn from them."

Darren agreed to undertake the Proverbs Project, as we called it. The next day, I returned to Dallas.

Eight weeks later I received a note from Darren stating, "Every morning after breakfast, Diana and I read a chapter in Proverbs. At first I thought, *Why did you give me this project? Nothing I've read so far has anything to do with anger.* But eventually, I saw what I needed to see. I needed a *new me.* I did what you suggested—I completed the Proverbs Project.

"When I read all the verses that show what an angry man looks like, I was overwhelmed by the image of the person I *did not* want to become—someone who stirs up strife and dissension, someone people should avoid. I knew I needed to change. Well, now the Lord is changing me!"

A short time later, I had dinner with Darren and Diana, who had come to Dallas on business. What a joy! Diana quickly confirmed, "It's made all the difference in the world!"

I was so grateful to God.

Since that time, I have "prescribed" the Proverbs Project to many a struggler. This exercise is usually not a cure-all—nor a quick fix—but it provides the motivation to want to cooperate with God, the motivation to allow Him to change anyone who is willing. The Bible says, "The one who calls you is faithful and he will do it" (1 Thessalonians 5:24).

How to Head Off Anger at the Pass

We demonstrate great wisdom when we determine, in advance, how to act rather than react: This means we *anticipate* what might happen when we get angry, and we *plan ahead* to keep things from getting out of hand. We prepare ahead of time for "quenching the coals" of heated episodes and therefore limit the potential destruction.

Let me offer four ways we can head off our anger at the pass:

1. Identify Your Triggers

All of us have certain situations that trigger our anger. Although a lot of things in life can make us mad, each of us has certain "recurring themes" when it comes to being provoked. That is, our anger episodes are usually caused by the same triggers over and over. Analyzing your anger patterns can help better move you from subjectivity to objectivity, from being controlled by anger to controlling it.

To identify your triggers, ask yourself the following questions:

- There are four sources of anger (hurt, injustice, fear, frustration). Is there one that tends to provoke my anger more than others?

- When I review your recent anger episodes, does a pattern emerge?

- What painful issues from my past, especially from childhood, stir up present-day emotions? What experiences from back *then* inflame anger here and *now*?

- Are there certain environments that seem to "conduct" my anger energy more than others (the workplace, family get-togethers, competitive events, neighborhood gatherings)?

- Is there a certain type of personality that tends to push my buttons (loud and bossy, quiet and conniving)? Why do I think this is so?

- If I could label the kinds of things that make me mad, what would they be? Think of at least three or four anger igniters (perhaps disrespect, manipulation, dishonesty, sarcasm, irresponsibility).

By thinking through these questions, you can gain keener insight into what activates your anger. By identifying your triggers, you can be proactive in dealing with them.

2. Train Your Brain

A key point in this book so far has been that denying or suppressing angry feelings is counterproductive. We must acknowledge and accept our emotions so that we can deal with them in a healthy way. This doesn't mean our feelings should trump logical thinking. We all know people who are ruled by unhealthy emotions, and it isn't a pretty picture. It's all about first acknowledging our emotions, then learning how to control them and use them for a beneficial purpose.

I am fascinated by how much God's Word has to say about our hearts and our minds, and how they are interrelated. Jesus told His followers to "love the Lord your God with all your heart and with all your soul and with all your mind."[1] And the psalmist wrote, "Test me, O LORD, and try me, examine my heart and my mind."[2]

I'm so grateful that God created us with the capacity to fulfill His desires and comply with His truth. Clearly, the Lord intends for both our thoughts and emotions to be used in conjunction with one another. Our hearts can be reshaped and our brains rewired so that our behaviors will become more and more Christlike.

That's why Paul said, "Do not conform any longer to the pattern of this world, but be transformed by the renewing of your mind. Then you will be able to test and approve what God's will is—his good, pleasing, and perfect will."[3] Peter said to "prepare your minds for action; be self-controlled."[4]

Understanding these and other scriptures is essential for those of us who want to change the way we handle anger. When we *train our brain*, we *change our behavior*.

One of the best ways to do this is by consistently studying and memorizing God's Word. Some people today question the value and necessity of Scripture memorization. After all, anyone with an Internet connection can look up Bible passages in a matter of seconds.

But gathering information about the Bible is just a small part of what God had in mind when He said, "How can a young person stay pure? By obeying your word...I have hidden your word in my heart that I might not sin against you."[5]

Jesus put the matter in straightforward terms: "The good man brings good things out of the good stored up in him, and the evil man brings evil things out of the evil stored up in him."[6] If we want to change our responses to anger, one of the best ways is by saturating our thoughts with the life-changing truths of God's Word.

3. Prepare an Anger Action Plan

All too frequently we read about another shooting at a school, a mall, or even a church. Because of this, many institutions have drawn up emergency action plans so that they'll know how to respond should a crisis occur.

> You will find it helpful to think through *in advance* the appropriate, productive response when your emotions get hot.

Let's take that idea and apply it to our anger. You will find it helpful to think through in advance the appropriate, productive response when your emotions get hot. Consider:

> *An appropriate action* is to cautiously express your thoughts and feelings with understanding and concern for the other person's welfare. Proverbs 17:27 says, "A man of knowledge uses words with restraint, and a man of understanding is even-tempered."

An inappropriate reaction is to express your thoughts and feelings in such a way that they stir up anger in others and produce strife. Proverbs 30:33 paints this graphic picture: "As churning the milk produces butter, and as twisting the nose produces blood, so stirring up anger produces strife."

While you're calm and unhurried, envision how you would like to respond the next time you get angry. You can start devising your individualized "anger action plan" by thinking carefully about how you want to respond in heated situations.

Consider the following:

Appropriate Actions	Inappropriate Reactions
Ask Yourself...	
Will I use tactful, compassionate words?	Will I use tactless, condemning words?
Will I try to see the other person's point of view?	Will I see only my point of view?
Will I want to help the one who angers me?	Will I want to punish the one who angers me?
Will I focus first on my own faults?	Will I focus only on the faults of others?
Will I have realistic expectations?	Will I have unrealistic expectations?
Will I have a flexible and cooperative attitude?	Will I have a rigid and uncooperative attitude?
Will I forgive personal injustices?	Will I avenge personal injustices?

4. Communicate Your Anger to Another

Learning how to convey anger appropriately will better help you put out the fires that could scorch your relationships.

Before communicating your anger toward someone, take time to evaluate whether expressing your anger is needful, appropriate, and will prove beneficial.

Some people simply do not know how to handle anger directed toward them. They become hostile and defensive, or weak and placating, resolving nothing.

If you simply want to vent your feelings, to release some pent-up steam, then pour out your heart to God and maybe to another person until or if you're led to confront your offender. Should you decide to arrange a meeting and confront the one who has angered you, here are some things to help you prepare:

Choose to be proactive
- Examine your motivation.
- Be realistic in your expectations.
- Know what you want to accomplish.
- Assess the legitimacy of your request.
- Rehearse how you will approach the subject.
- Anticipate possible reactions from the other person.
- Think through how you might respond to those reactions.
- Decide whether you are willing to live with any negative repercussions.
- Talk with a wise and trusted person if you are uncertain what to do.

Choose a time and place to talk
- Select a time and place convenient for both of you; find an atmosphere conducive for listening and sharing.
- Meet on "neutral turf" so both of you are likely to feel a sense of equality in tackling difficult subject matters.
- Allot sufficient time for both of you to address your concerns.

- Commit the time to God and seek His wisdom and guidance. Communicate your desires for open and honest communication and resolution.

- Express your pain and anger in a loving, nonaccusatory way, utilizing the "sandwich technique" (see pages 66-67).

- Evaluate the willingness of your offender to receive your confrontation without becoming angry or defensive while understanding your hurt, fear, frustration, or indignation over an injustice.

- Give opportunity for a response without interruption or defensiveness on your part.

- Affirm what is being said by repeating and clarifying spoken statements.

- Request any desired changes in behavior you believe will resolve the present problem and prevent future problems.

- Agree to change any problematic behavior on your part.

- Promote fairness and objectivity, openness and optimism.

- Extend total forgiveness unreservedly and willingly.

- Value differences in goals, desires, and priorities.

- Applaud the person's willingness to listen to you, to resolve the problem, and to work toward improving your relationship.

Always keep this in mind: "A word aptly spoken is like apples of gold in settings of silver."[7]

I also recommend creating a written outline or plan of the way you want to think and act when hurt, injustice, fear, or frustration come your way—a series of steps to deal with the inevitable sources of anger that each of us struggle with.

Consider...how exactly can you respond in a godly way? What will you avoid doing? How can you remain calm and clearheaded? What is the optimal outcome for a conflict? (If you have trouble developing a plan, remember that chapter 13 outlines a process for alleviating present anger. These steps will provide a framework you can apply to your individual situation and anger temperament.)

Jesus encouraged us to plan ahead. He said,

> *"Suppose one of you wants to build a tower.*
> *Will he not first sit down and estimate the cost to see*
> *if he has enough money to complete it?...*
> *Or suppose a king is about to go to war against another king.*
> *Will he not first sit down and consider whether*
> *he is able with ten thousand men to oppose the one coming*
> *against him with twenty thousand?"*
> (Luke 14:28,31).

Don't wait until you're in the heat of battle to figure out how to respond. Sit down now and create an "anger action plan" before the moment of need arrives.

Surrender Yourself to God's Healing

In the mid-1800s, a woman named Frances Ridley Havergal authored more than 70 beloved hymns, including "Take My Life and Let It Be" and "Like a River Glorious," as well as numerous volumes of poetry and devotional works. During her lifetime, Frances was widely popular and greatly admired. She was one of the most creative and devout Christians of her era. Even today her hymns are sung in churches throughout the world.

Here's something else, though, about Frances: She had a very bad temper—the kind characterized as *explosive*. After her anger eruptions, she would be mortified and confess her wrongdoing to the Lord. But then she would lose her temper again...and again.

One day after a particularly bad explosion, she threw herself down by her bed and wept. She prayed, "Lord, must it always be so? Will I always have this temper to keep me humble before You?"

While she was on her knees, the Lord planted a verse in her mind: "The Egyptians whom you have seen today you will see no more forever." Initially mystified as to the meaning of God's message, Frances then remembered God's speaking these words to Moses when the Egyptians pursued the Israelites to take them back into bondage.

She applied the verse to her own situation by equating the Egyptians to her temper and the way in which Satan wanted to use it to keep her in bondage. She had never doubted God's ability to free her, but now she realized God not only *could* free her, but *would* free her. He was going to take her temper away.

Brimming over with joy, Frances boldly asked, "Lord, could it be forever?"

It seemed to her the words came back from the Lord, "Yes. No more...forever."

Frances's sister said from that day on, Frances never again lost her temper. She believed God, and God did a miracle.[8] Anger was never a problem for Frances again.

※

If we want to change the way we deal with anger, let's first go to God with humble and contrite hearts, asking Him to heal us, change our hurtful behavior, and conform us to the character of Christ. The Bible says, "The righteous cry out, and the LORD hears them; he delivers them from all their troubles. The LORD is close to the brokenhearted and saves those who are crushed in spirit" (Psalm 34:17-18).

God may choose to bring instant change, as He did with Frances. Or He may cause growth and transformation over a period of time, which more often seems to be the case. Either way, when we surrender our lives to the Lord, we can be assured He'll work powerfully *within* us to make us like Christ and *through* us to show Christ to others.

The Refiner's Fire

How to Respond to Blowups by Setting Boundaries

"You, O God, tested us; you refined us like silver"
(PSALM 66:10).

THE SETTING: JERUSALEM. The time: 1000 BC.

Silas the silversmith closely examines the rough ore before him—silver tainted with zinc, copper, and tin. He anticipates the amazing change soon to take place—taking a chunk of rock with little or no value and transforming it into the purest silver. Silas is a superb craftsman, skilled at separating the impurities from the silver, skilled at surfacing dross and removing it.

Silas knows it will take heat—varying degrees of intense heat—to purge the dross from the silver. This purification process will forever change the composition of the rough rock. But first he must hammer it, break it, and grind it so that he can place it in a crucible.

His clay crucible—the impenetrable pot that withstands the highest degrees of heat—is placed over a fire. The ore melts, and a layer of dross forms on the surface. Patiently, Silas waits and watches...then skims off the impurities. Eventually, he looks down into the pot and gazes upon a dim image—his own image—yet still a dull reflection. The liquefied mass still lacks purity. So after raising the heat even higher, the refiner carefully places the crucible back into the blistering furnace.

It's a process the expert silversmith will repeat as long as necessary;

he is doggedly determined to remove all of the dross. Silas knows the refining is completely finished when he sees a clear image, a perfect reflection of himself, in the molten ore. This will signify the silver has attained the highest degree of purity possible.

Like the silversmiths of old, God is a Master Refiner. In Jeremiah 9:7 we read, "The LORD Almighty says: 'See, I will refine and test them.'" But it's His children, not chunks of ore, that He seeks to purify. And there is a distinct image He, too, is yearning to see. Only after spending considerable time *in the crucible*—only after the Refiner continues to remove our dross—can we be purified. He loves to look upon us and see a clearer reflection—a shining reflection of Christ.

My personal experiences in the crucible have been incredibly intense —but also helpful, and even more so, healing.

Finding Faulty Thinking

When it comes to getting angry—red-hot angry—it takes a *whole lot* to "light my fire." I attribute that to spending so many years fearfully sidestepping anger—both mine and everyone else's. People who know me say I have a long, long fuse.

Yet on one occasion some years back, my five-mile-long fuse was snipped off to five millimeters—and quickly lit. My emotions exploded. In my mind's eye I saw bright red—crimson red, fiery red! Let me further paint the picture for you...

We can all look back and identify a few people who, in one way or another, made huge contributions to our lives. God brought them into our lives to teach us profound lessons and to refine us. They were key players He then moved from center stage into the wings, or even out the exit doors of our lives.

"Meg" was one such significant person in my life. I never suspected our relationship would enter the Refiner's fire. Linked together at a Christian music conference, we clicked almost immediately. Smart, talented, and superb with lyrics, Meg quickly gained my admiration and almost as quickly became a trusted confidant.

We also spent more and more time together brainstorming and

planning. We talked openly, sharing our struggles, experiences, and aspirations. We often prayed together, asking God for His blessing. We were riding a wave of enthusiasm, clinging to high hopes and close-knit hearts.

Or so it seemed…

Poisoning the Well

One day Meg suggested we employ "Paula," a young, bright, and gifted woman whose talents I also truly admired. But I was surprised at the suggestion and somewhat skeptical, for good reason. Paula had resented my friendship with Meg and had given me the silent treatment for years.

Meg really wanted Paula on board, so hesitantly I agreed, and for well over a year everything ran smoothly.

Then I began to sense Meg distancing herself from me. Several times I asked about it, but each time she brushed my concern aside. I still, however, couldn't shake my troubled feelings. Something just didn't seem right. *What had happened? What had changed her?*

One day as Paula was talking with me, a startling realization hit me. Finally, I saw what had been happening to my heart-connection with Meg. All the negative phrases I'd been hearing—uncharacteristically—from her, I now heard coming from Paula's lips. Suddenly I thought, *So that's where Meg's getting it. Paula has "poisoned the well."*

Two months later, Paula came to me and said, very directly, "I want you to know I'm really supportive of your friendship with Meg. I want what is best for both of you. I know there has been a strain between the two of you, but I want your relationship healed."

At that moment, I felt so grateful, so relieved. Her words of affirmation—so meaningful—were spoken at Meg's home after the three of us had completed one of our marathon work sessions.

The Card That Caused a Kaboom

Meg and Paula then left to pick up a late dinner. I stayed behind to continue working. After making a few photocopies, I walked back to our large, shared office area. But rather than going to my desk for paper clips, I stopped at Meg's, which was closer to the copier.

When I opened Meg's desk drawer I noticed Paula's handwriting on a card she had given to Meg. Like a magnet, my eyes fell upon *my name*, then fixated on one line: "We don't need any more June Hunts in this world." *What? I couldn't believe it…the unkindness, the outright cruelty!* This was the match that lit my fuse—and instantly ignited a powder keg of emotion.

I was stunned…hurt…and *very, very angry.* Just an hour earlier—*just one hour*—Paula had looked me straight in the eye and declared, "June, I'm really *for* you. I want to *help* you. I want to *support* you and your relationship with Meg."

To this day, it's as if the words on that card have been seared into my mind with a hot branding iron. I felt utterly manipulated and deceived, maligned and betrayed.

Fury coursed through my body, adrenaline pumped through my veins. I knew if I didn't find a way to reduce the temperature of my boiling anger, I would explode at my "friend."

To prevent saying what I would later regret, I needed to leave—*immediately!*

I have to get out of here! I thought. *Jogging will release all this steam and cool me down.* Abruptly gathering my things, I scribbled a note to Meg that something had come up and I had to leave. Then I bolted out the door.

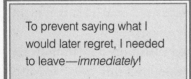

To prevent saying what I would later regret, I needed to leave—*immediately!*

As soon as I returned to my home, I laced up my running shoes—tighter than normal—and hurried outside.

I was ready to "run off" my rage. (At that time, I customarily did a two-mile trek—a run-walk-run routine.)

A few minutes into my run, I noticed my arms swinging higher than normal—intensely, vigorously, aggressively. I remember thinking, *How unusual!*

However, even after 20 minutes of running, *I felt no relief.* I had expected the physical exertion to be my anger-reducer—like the valve that releases the steam inside a pressure cooker. But it didn't work. My valve seemed to be stuck! In fact, the longer I jogged, the more pressure I felt.

From Rehearsal to Reversal

Soon I realized *why* there was no relief. The Bible makes it clear, "Love...keeps no record of wrongs."[1] Keeps no record! That's the very thing—the *only* thing I had been doing! Over and over, I had been rehearsing how much I had been wronged, how much I had been betrayed.

And the more I did it, the more difficult it became *not* to do it. This much was certain: All that "rehearsing" wasn't helping! The fire roaring inside me continued to rage. And no wonder—you can't put out a fire by continuing to fuel it!

I remember thinking, *I've got to do something else! Lord, teach me to act rather than react.* I repeated those words again and again. Soon I was rhythmically praying, right in sync with my running stride, over and over: "Teach me to act rather than react...teach me to act rather than react."

By the end of my hour-long jog, my pounding heart was finally at peace. I was no longer controlled by the debilitating sense of betrayal. Of course, the initial problem had yet to be confronted, but that night I successfully released all my anger to the Lord.

The next day, when I confronted Meg about the note from Paula, I have to admit my anger was sparked again. But this time I was able to control the fire, rather than let the fire control me. I was not consumed by its explosive heat as I had been the night before.

At the time, the intensity of my initial anger shocked me—it was unusual for me to get *so* angry *so* fast. In retrospect, I realize I had experienced the four sources of anger (hurt, injustice, fear, frustration)—not just one at a time, but all at once! Although it was Paula who undermined me on that card, I had to face the fact that it was my close friend Meg who chose to keep Paula's card rather than discard it.

Although the Lord eventually moved Meg out of my life, He used this experience in His refining fire to remove more of my dross. He intended to purify me, and this wouldn't be the last time I would be found in the Refiner's fire.

> When you find yourself becoming angry, pray, "Lord, teach me to act rather than react."

Yet ever since that day, when I feel a strong surge of anger, *if*—and I do mean *if*—I sincerely pray, "Lord, teach me to act rather than react," God gives me the wisdom to carefully weigh my words and to speak with self-control.

And my heart is soon at peace.

Lessons Learned in the Furnace

Years ago, I found a picture in both the Old and New Testaments that helped me—more than anything else—to make sense of my personal pain.

The Bible says of God, "He will sit as a refiner and purifier of silver,"[2] and He sees us as unrefined silver. As our Refiner, He first places us into a crucible, then puts the crucible into the furnace—the furnace of affliction—not to punish us, but to purify us.

In a parallel way, God saw me as rough ore that needed much refining. By putting pressure on me through my experience with Meg and Paula, I became finely ground so that He could fit me into His crucible. Of course, I was totally unaware of all the impurities within me—impurities that took a long time for me to see.

Not long after this "visit" in the furnace when Meg distanced herself from me, the Refiner reheated the furnace to His desired temperature and put me back in the crucible. I was in the sweltering furnace and I definitely wanted out, but instead, the Refiner was lovingly determined to remove more dross. *And even more dross...*

Because certain impurities are released only at extremely high temperatures, it took that card—with its caustic message—to bring to the surface impurities deeply embedded in me.

The subsequent dross I didn't see was my being too emotionally dependent upon Meg—assuming she was "essential" to my life—and fearing I would be abandoned. With the dross removed, I saw that my deepest dependence needed to always be on Jesus, and that He would never abandon me.

The Bible promises, "The LORD himself goes before you and will be with you; he will never leave you nor forsake you. Do not be afraid; do not be discouraged."[3] What assurance, what comfort!

Anger Hits Home, Relatively Speaking

There would be more for me to learn about how to deal with anger, including anger directed *toward me*. The image the Master Refiner saw in my crucible must have still been muddy. So, exit Meg and enter "Peg" for another bout in the blazing heat.

Peg is an endearing relative I didn't know well while I was growing up because she was raised in another state. But when she moved to Dallas, we became instant friends.

Growing Concerns

Despite Peg's many wonderful qualities, she was, at times, controlling. Given my tendency to be an *anger avoider* and my former "need" to be a *peace-at-all-costs person*, I often allowed her to control me.

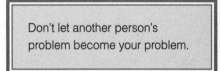

Don't let another person's problem become your problem.

Sometimes Peg would call me on the phone and start yelling at me. On one occasion, I was a guest speaker at a conference in Kansas. I was summoned from the hotel ballroom to a kitchen phone. After I said "Hello," Peg began yelling accusations. No matter what my explanation, she refused to accept the truth. I was left stymied and stunned. And that was just one of many calls.

Increasingly, Peg became disrespectful. Several people conveyed negative comments she had made about me. A few people asked, "June, why do you take it? Why don't you stand up for yourself? You shouldn't let her control you." Hard as it was for me to admit, they were right.

Building Boundaries

When Peg acted angrily toward me, I knew I needed to get my brain in gear by guarding my thoughts and emotions. I developed the following three-step process:

1. *I prayed for God's protection.* Psalm 141:3 says, "Set a guard over my mouth, O LORD; keep watch over the door of my lips." I submitted my mouth to the Refiner.

2. *I corrected my thinking* by saying to myself, not her, "She has a problem. I'm not going to let her problem be my problem." I submitted my mind to the Refiner.

3. *I set boundaries* with a *repercussion* and a *reward*. I submitted my will to the Refiner.

I had always been intimidated by anger, feared being abandoned, and doubted God's promise to meet my emotional needs (deeply embedded impurities only the Refiner could see). These were difficult truths to swallow, but I was committed to being a person of integrity so I had to face them to become the person God created me to be.

How well I remember establishing my first boundary with Peg. I laid down the groundwork with these words (and I've included her basic responses):

- "Do you want us to have the best relationship possible?" ("Yes.")

- "Do you believe that we are truly encouraging each other?" ("No.")

- "In a close relationship, both people should be better because of each other. Do you agree?" ("Yes, I do.")

- "Peg, I value our friendship and want us to encourage each

other. But when anger explodes, it hurts both of us."
(*"I agree."*)

- "I don't want to fear you; I want to enjoy you. So, in the future, if either one of us has destructive anger, we need to step back and part from each other for a while so that the anger doesn't damage our relationship further."

Peg said she understood, but of course, the boundary hadn't yet been tested. I knew that the next time we related negatively, it would be best for us to distance ourselves for awhile. And that day came within a week.

On that day, I arrived at Peg's home—30 minutes later than planned because of an important phone call—and as soon as she saw me she began yelling, "Where have you been?!"

When Peg's temper flared, I followed my previously prepared plan of action. (I had repeatedly rehearsed each point until I could confidently and calmly communicate each one.) I reminded her of our previous agreement, but she kept up her angry criticism.

Instead of *talking* with me, Peg exploded at me, *telling* me what I was thinking, which wasn't even close to the truth. She continued for several minutes, and I thought, *No more.*

Holding up my hand (palm toward her), I said, "Stop!" To my astonishment, she did—she stopped!

Speaking slowly in a low voice I said, "Obviously now is not a good time for us to be together." Again, slowly, lowly, and deliberately, I said, "I'm going to leave."

Surprised, Peg said, "You can't leave."

I responded, "This conversation isn't encouraging either of us, so I need to leave. Later on we can try again." I returned home and was grateful and amazed that I had set a boundary and kept it!

Disengage from Rage

Now, whenever I sense self-control giving way to irrational anger—whether in me or in others—I know it's time to put on the brakes, call a truce, and take a time-out. Heated conversations will only escalate unless we do something to intervene in the process. Here's what I do:

- *I hold up my hands to indicate I am "surrendering"* for the time being by calling a halt to what is taking place.
  —"Stop! Time-out!"
  —"Wait! We need to start over!"

- *I state slowly in a low tone of voice* (remember, "sloooow and loooow"):
  —"Our conversation isn't going in a positive direction."
  —"We won't be able to resolve anything this way."

- *I explain my need to disengage from the person who is angry* by taking a walk around the block, retreating to a quiet place, listening to music, taking a shower, or doing whatever I think will help me and/or the other person cool down and regain composure.
  —"I'm going to leave for a while."
  —"I will be back later"…(if that's wise).

- *I agree on a time to resume the conversation* when we can both talk calmly.
  —"When is a good time for us to discuss this?"
  —"Where can we meet with no distractions?"

If we reach an impasse where agreement is not possible, we can:

- *Agree to disagree by allowing different opinions* but not letting that become a problem.
  —*Decide to engage in stimulating conversations* where varied opinions are expressed (consider them opportunities to develop

listening skills, glean insights, process opinions, and express thoughts clearly and concisely in a nonoffensive way).

—*Commit to valuing and respecting* each other and growing in understanding of one another. Proverbs 18:2 says, "A fool finds no pleasure in understanding but delights in airing his own opinions."

Different Dynamics, Different Tactics

My newfound dedication to constructively expressing my anger through boundaries shifted the dynamics of my relationship with Peg. It's true there were other times when Peg would get angry at me. But once I learned to hold the line—*and not have to have her approval*—a major change occurred. Over a span of many months, our relationship moved from negative to positive.

When I felt fear welling up in me concerning my relationship with Peg, I claimed God's promises to meet my deepest inner needs for love, significance, and security. The Bible says, "My God will meet all your needs according to his glorious riches in Christ Jesus."[4]

Have you ever noticed that many people were angry at Jesus, but He wasn't controlled by their anger? He knew they had a problem, but He didn't let their problem become His problem. When I thought about Him, that helped me.

In a relatively short time, I was amazed at the change within me. (I learned that *not* being controlled by someone's anger is truly life-changing.) And much of what I learned came from forays in the fire.

By expressing my feelings—even anger—in a caring and productive way and challenging Peg to do the same, I gained new courage and confidence which, in turn, resulted in unmistakable improvements in us both. Over time, Peg softened and learned to communicate without harsh words. Today our friendship has become more and more refined and we recognize how the Refiner has brought healing—not only to us individually, but also to our relationship. What a joy!

As I applied my newly honed skills to situations at work and in other relationships, God repeatedly proved His faithfulness to me, and now my security truly rests in Him alone! Although I'm still a work in progress, a lot of dross has been drawn away for good.

> The Refiner has but one goal in mind: to turn you into a masterpiece, something that shines with lasting beauty.

Although we will all experience fiery trials, not everyone is willing to learn from their trials. The book of Jeremiah refers to certain people—"they are called rejected silver."[5] They have hardened their hearts, rejecting the purifying work of God in their lives. What sad words from the Master Refiner: "The bellows blow fiercely to burn away the lead with fire, but the refining goes on in vain" (Jeremiah 6:29).

As you feel the heat of refining fires in your own life, don't allow yourself to be characterized as "rejected silver" because you are clamoring to climb out of the crucible and refusing to submit to the purifying flames. Remember, the Refiner has but one goal in mind: to turn you into a masterpiece, something that shines with lasting beauty.

※

Atop my desk is a rectangular block of silver—a reminder of how God purifies me in His refining fire. This small bar has been designed, shaped, and cooled, having completed its rigorous purification process.

Process...oh yes, it is most definitely a process! I look at my silver bar and remember my frequent visits in the furnace of affliction, my containment in the crucible, and my desperately wanting out. Yet today I'm grateful and say, "Thank You, Father, for all that I've learned through these trials...through Your purifying fire." My silver bar is a reminder that as long as I live on this earth, I will experience times of purposeful pain.

You also have a choice of how to respond. You can either become *rejected* silver or *refined* silver. And instead of staying angry about your pain, realize that the pathway to your purification is purposeful pain.

Because being purified like silver is a *process*, you are a work in *progress*—you are God's work. His fire of purification will never result in harm *to* you, but will merely clear away what is worthless *in* you...so that the countenance of Christ can shine *through* you.

Are you in the crucible right now? Take comfort—the Refiner knows you. He cares for you; He loves you.

Just as the silversmith waits ever present during the entire refining process, so our Lord is ever present with you. Intently, He sits with you and watches over you. His eyes are locked on what is happening to you. His tender love will not allow Him to look away—not even for an instant.

In Zechariah 13:9, God says, "I will refine them like silver and test them like gold." When you come under the care of the Master Refiner and consent to being in His crucible, you will more and more reflect the character of Christ. You will shine like silver...you will glitter like gold.

Epilogue: The Fire Extinguisher

How to Act Rather Than React

*"Don't sin by letting anger control you.
Think about it overnight and remain silent"*
(PSALM 4:4 NLT).

SO OFTEN I'VE thought about the time of my short-fuse explosion...my futile effort to run off my rage...and the simple prayer that brought me peace: "Lord, teach me to act rather than react." I remember that volatile evening when I walked into my bedroom with those words reverberating in my mind—in rhythm—and thinking, *That could make a memorable song.*

Within three days, I had written the words and the music. Even though it was borne out of trials and tears, every time I sing it before an audience, it seems to cause a smile, lighten a load, lift a heart. *And my sincere prayer is that it will do the same for you...*that God will use it to help you find the answer to anger.

Isn't it interesting that nothing is wasted when released into the care of the Refiner—released as a sacrificial offering, released to reflect the character of Christ?

Lord, Teach Me to Act Rather Than React

(Rhythmic, country style)

Chorus

    Lord, teach me to act rather than react,
        with Your Spirit in control of me.
    Lord, teach me to help rather than hinder,
        with the Lord being Lord of me.
    Lord, teach me to trust rather than mistrust,
        with Your Spirit inside my soul.
    Lord, teach me to act rather than react,
        I give You complete control.

Verse 1

    It was stop-and-go traffic, the scene was so graphic,
        When headin' back home from town.
    A car was behind me, and then pulled beside me,
        The driver had a serious frown.
    He looked straight at me, it was plain to see,
        He was forcin' his way around.
    I said, "No, you won't! Oh, no you don't!"
        Then pushed my foot to the ground. Oh...

Chorus

Verse 2

    It was quarter to 3:00 for the luncheon with Lee—
        But the meetin' was planned at 1:00!
    This had happened before, so my feelin's were sore,
        Now this was not my picture of fun.
    Lee came in with a grin—no repentance within—
        Civil war had just begun.
    I was feelin' rejection, and voiced my objection,
        "You selfish son of a gun!" Oh...

Chorus

Verse 3 (Slow, half time)

> When I feel disappointment, with no soothing ointment,
>> And nothin' is goin' my way.
> When my heart has been breaking, and my soul is aching,
>> And I have no more words to say.
> I'm not under illusion, the only solution,
>> Is to die to my rights each day.
> Because Christ is inside me to comfort and guide me,
>> And His life has taught me to pray…

Chorus (slow, half time)

> Lord, teach me to act rather than react,
>> with Your Spirit in control of me.
> Lord, teach me to help rather than hinder,
>> with the Lord being Lord of me.
> Lord, teach me to trust rather than mistrust,
>> with Your Spirit inside my soul.
> Lord, teach me to act rather than react,
>> I give You complete…
>>> I won't take defeat…I give You complete control.*

---

* To hear June sing "Lord, Teach Me to Act Rather Than React,"
  visit http:www.hopefortheheart.org/Anger.

Notes

Chapter 1—The Anger Bowl

1. Frank Minirth et al., *Love Hunger* (Nashville: Thomas Nelson, 1990), p. 13.

2. American Psychiatric Association, *Diagnostic and Statistical Manual of Mental Disorders: DSM-III-R,* 3d ed. (Washington, DC: American Psychiatric Association, 1987), pp. 65-67.

3. 2 Samuel 24:24.

4. 1 Peter 5:7.

Chapter 2—Turning Up the Heat

1. Proverbs 20:2.

2. Ray Burwick, *The Menace Within: Hurt or Anger?* (Birmingham, AL: Ray Burwick, 1985), p. 18; Gary D. Chapman, *The Other Side of Love: Handling Anger in a Godly Way* (Chicago: Moody, 1999), pp. 17-18.

3. W.E. Vine, *Vine's Complete Expository Dictionary of Biblical Words*, electronic ed. (Nashville: Thomas Nelson, 1996).

4. Proverbs 22:24.

5. Matthew 26:4.

6. Mark 10:14.

7. Romans 1:18.

8. A.W. Tozer, from the *Alliance Weekly,* July 1946.

9. Acts 5:33.

10. Proverbs 27:4.

11. Proverbs 19:3.

12. Romans 8:28 NKJV.

13. Ecclesiastes 7:9.

14. Proverbs 29:8.

Chapter 3—Fuel for the Fire

1. Proverbs 23:7 KJV.

2. Charles Dickens, *Great Expectations* (Whitefish, MT: Kessinger Publishing, 2004), p. 60.

3. 1 John 4:18.

Chapter 4—Ashes to Ashes

1. Proverbs 6:27.

2. Matthew 6:34.

3. John T. Slania, "Putting Violence Policies to Work; System Can Help Prevent Tragedies," *Crain's Chicago Business*, February 19, 2001.

4. Psalm 37:8-9.

5. Gary Bousman, "Anger: It Can Be Like Slow-Acting Poison, Robbing You of Mental and Physical Health," *Vibrant Life*, July 1, 1995.

6. Rachel Lampert, M.D., et al., "Anger-Induced T-Wave Alternans Predicts Future Ventricular Arrythmias in Patients with Implantable Cardioverter-Defibrillators," *Journal of the American College of Cardiology*, March 3, 2009, pp. 774-78.

7. Renee C. Lee, "Anger in Men Has Link to Strokes," *Charleston Gazette*, March 2, 2004.

8. Daniel Goleman, "Study Documents How Anger Can Impair Heart Function," *The New York Times*, September 2, 1992.

9. Goleman, "Study," *The New York Times*.

10. Troy Goodman, "Study: Anger Triggers Heart Attacks," *The Cincinnati Post*, May 2, 2000.

11. Alan Sherzagier, "Hospital Research Discovers Anger Raises Risk of Injury," *Deseret News* (Salt Lake City), February 2, 2006 (emphasis added).

12. Nicole Walker, "Why Anger Is Bad for Your Health," *Jet*, May 1, 2000.

13. James 1:19-20.

14. Joseph Carey, *Brain Facts: A Primer on the Brain and Nervous* System, 5th ed. (Washington, DC: Society for Neuroscience, 2006), pp. 29-30. Retrieved June 2, 2008 from http://www.sfn.org/skins/main/pdf/brainfacts/brainfacts.pdf.

15. Philippians 4:6.

16. Philippians 4:7.

17. Matthew 11:28-29.

18. Ephesians 4:26-27.

19. Matthew 5:44.

20. 1 John 5:3.

21. 2 Corinthians 5:17.

22. Romans 12:18.

Chapter 5—The Fire Eaters

1. Ephesians 4:26-27.

2. Marcia L. Conner, James G. Clawson, *Creating a Learning Culture* (Cambridge University Press, 2004), p. 328.

3. Albert Einstein, as quoted in Ronald J. Comer, *Abnormal Psychology*, 5th ed. (New York: Macmillan, 2003), p. 5.

4. Deuteronomy 32:35.

5. Romans 12:17.

6. Proverbs 15:1.

7. Romans 8:33-34.

Chapter 6—The Flamethrowers

1. Much of this story is adapted from Mike Barber, "Crotchety Harry Truman Remains an Icon of the Eruption," *Seattle Post-Intelligencer Reporter,* May 11, 2000. Accessed at http://seattlepi.nwsource.com/mountsthelens/hary11.shtml.

2. William Safire, *Safire's Political Dictionary* (New York: Oxford University Press, 2008), p. 348.

3. Donna duBeth, "Give 'em Hell, Harry," *The Daily News*, March 26, 1980. Accessed at http://www.tdn.com/helens/flash/mainpage.php?p=1113365891&w=D.

4. For information on the Mount St. Helen's eruption, see "Mt. St. Helen's Eruption, 1980," http://www.geology.sdsu.edu/how_volcanoes_work/Sthelens.html.

5. Proverbs 22:24.

6. ESV.

7. Frederick Buechner, *Beyond Words* (San Francisco: HarperSanFrancisco, 2004), p. 18.

8. Hebrews 12:15.

9. Matthew 5:25.

10. 1 John 1:8-10 NLT.

11. John 8:32.

12. L. Heise, M. Ellsberg, and M. Gottemoeller, "Ending Violence Against Women," *Population Reports*, Series L, no. 11 (Baltimore, MD: Johns Hopkins University School of Public Health, December 1999), p. 1.

13. The Commonwealth Fund, *Health Concerns Across a Woman's Lifespan* (Rochester, NY: Louis Harris and Associates, May 1999), p. 27.

14. E. Cohen and J. Knitzer, "Children Living with Domestic Violence," a report prepared for "Early Childhood, Domestic Violence, and Poverty: Taking the Next Steps to Help Young Children and Their Families," May 2002, as cited in *National Task Force to End Sexual and Domestic Violence Against Women*, "Violence Against Women Act 2005, Title IV-Prevention."

15. 2 Corinthians 7:10-11.

16. James 5:16.

Chapter 7—Blast from the Past

1. Gary Chapman, *Anger: Handling a Powerful Emotion in a Healthy Way* (Chicago, IL: Northfield Publishing, 2007), p. 99.

Chapter 8—Too Hot to Handle

1. Matthew 7:12.

2. Martin Luther King and Coretta Scott King, *The Martin Luther King, Jr. Companion: Quotations from the Speeches, Essays, and Books of Martin Luther King, Jr.* (New York: Macmillan, 1993), p. 56.

Chapter 9—Fire and Ice

1. 1 Samuel 20:34.
2. Luke 10:40.
3. Luke 10:41-42.
4. Matthew 6:25.
5. Matthew 6:27.
6. Matthew 11:28-30.
7. Proverbs 15:1.
8. Louis Lalleman, Jean-Pierre de Caussade, and Claude De La Colombiere, *For God's Greater Glory: Gems of Jesuit Spirituality*, Jean-Pierre Lafouge, ed. (Bloomington, IN: World Wisdom, 2006), p. 71.

Chapter 10—Self-Inflicted Flames

1. 1 John 1:9.
2. William Joseph Federer, *America's God and Country: Encyclopedia of Quotations* (St. Louis, MO: Amerisearch, 1994), p. 294.
3. James 1:12.
4. Jeremiah 29:11.
5. Isaiah 59:2.
6. Romans 3:23.
7. Romans 6:23.
8. See 2 Peter 3:9.
9. Romans 5:8.
10. See John 10:18 and Matthew 20:28.
11. John 14:6.
12. Philippians 4:13.
13. John 7:38.
14. 1 Corinthians 15:34.
15. James 4:10.
16. Ezekiel 11:19.
17. John 5:24.
18. See Isaiah 61:3.

Chapter 11—Fuming at the Father

1. "Man 'Angry at God' Drives Minivan into Church Sanctuary," Catholic News Agency, February 21, 2008. Additional background information: Hudson Sangree, "Minivan Plows into Church," *Sacramento Bee*, February 21, 2008.
2. Job 23:2-4.
3. Genesis 3:1.

4. Genesis 3:4-5.

5. James 1:17.

6. 1 John 1:9.

7. Psalm 116:5.

8. Daniel 4:35.

9. Mark 14:34-36 ESV.

10. Luke 22:42.

11. Romans 8:28.

Chapter 12—Smoldering Embers

1. See also Ronald T. Potter-Efron, *Angry All the Time: An Emergency Guide to Anger Control*, 2d ed. (Oakland, CA: New Harbinger, 2005).

2. William H. Walton as quoted in Charles Gerber, *Healing for a Bitter Heart* (Joplin, MO: College Press, 1996), p. 74.

Chapter 13—Let Cooler Heads Prevail

1. 1 Peter 1:13; 3:8-9.

2. Psalm 26:2.

3. 2 Corinthians 10:5.

4. 1 Chronicles 28:9.

5. On the three God-given inner needs, see Lawrence J. Crabb, Jr., *Understanding People: Deep Longings for Relationship* (Grand Rapids: Zondervan, 1987), pp. 15-16; Robert S. McGee, *The Search for Significance*, 2d ed. (Houston, TX: Rapha, 1990), pp. 27-30.

6. Philippians 4:19.

7. Psalm 118:6.

8. Philippians 2:3-4.

9. John 16:13.

10. Philippians 4:7.

11. Proverbs 21:29.

12. Ecclesiastes 3:1,7.

13. Colossians 4:6.

Chapter 14—Creative Combustion

1. Romans 12:2 ESV.

2. See Richard W. Etulain, *César Chávez* (New York: Macmillan, 2002), p. 117.

3. Peter Matthiessen, *Sal si puedes (Escape if you can): César Chávez and the New American Revolution* (Berkeley, CA: University of California Press, 2000), p. x.

4. Dan La Botz, *César Chávez and La Causa* (New York: Longman, 2005), p. 175.

Chapter 15—Bomb Squad Basics

1. Ephesians 4:30-31.

2. Ephesians 5:22.

3. Marie M. Fortune, *Keeping the Faith: Questions and Answers for the Abused Woman* (San Francisco: Harper & Row, 1991), pp. 28-29.

4. See Kay Marshall Strom, *In the Name of Submission* (Portland, OR: Multnomah Publishers, 1985), p. 56.

5. See Strom, *In the Name of Submission*, pp. 56-58.

6. Matthew 7:9-11.

7. See 1 Peter 1:6-7.

8. Ephesians 4:2-3 ESV.

9. John Cook, as cited in *The Book of Positive Quotations*, Steve Deger and Leslie Ann Gibson, eds. (Minneapolis: Fairview Press, 2007), p. 261.

Chapter 16—Quenching the Coals

1. Matthew 22:37.

2. Psalm 26:2.

3. Romans 12:2.

4. 1 Peter 1:13.

5. Psalm 119:9,11 NLT.

6. Matthew 12:35.

7. Proverbs 25:11.

8. This story was adapted from J. Oswald Sanders, "How Do You Love?" *Discipleship Journal*, March/April 1981. To learn more about the life of the great hymn writer and poet, see *Frances Ridley Havergal: A Full Sketch of Her Life* by Edward Davies and *Memorials of Frances Ridley Havergal* by Maria Vernon Graham Havergal (her sister).

Chapter 17—The Refiner's Fire

1. 1 Corinthians 13:4-5.

2. Malachi 3:3.

3. Deuteronomy 31:8.

4. Philippians 4:19.

5. Jeremiah 6:30.

More Harvest House Books
by June Hunt

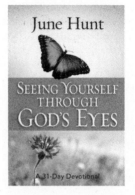

SEEING YOURSELF THROUGH GOD'S EYES

How well do you know your "identity" as a true Christian? Discover the great riches of your identity in the 31 devotions in this book. For example:

• I am adopted by God.

• I am a child of God.

• I am precious to God.

Experience the exciting transformation that comes from seeing yourself through God's eyes. Great for personal or group Bible study (Leader's Guide included).

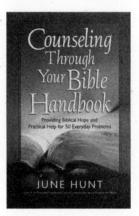

COUNSELING THROUGH YOUR BIBLE HANDBOOK

No matter what the problem, God doesn't leave us without hope or help. The Bible is richly relevant when it comes to the difficult dilemmas we all face. Here you will find 50 chapters of spiritual wisdom and compassionate counsel on even the hardest issues, such as...

• anger & adultery
• fear & phobias
• alcohol & drug abuse
• guilt & grief
• codependency & cults
• rejection & rape
• depression & dating
• self-worth & suicide

The guidance in this handbook is grounded in Scripture which—when used properly—has the power to pull us out of life's ditches and put us on the road to inner freedom and fulfillment. (Also available in hardback only from Hope For The Heart.)

HOW TO FORGIVE...
WHEN YOU DON'T FEEL LIKE IT

When someone hurts us, our natural response is to strike back. Rather than forgive, we want to return the pain and suffering. Rather than let go, we cling to our rocks of resentment, our boulders of bitterness. The result? We struggle under the weight of our grievances—all because we find it too hard to forgive.

Though we know God has called us to forgive, we find ourselves asking hard questions:

- What if it hurts too much to forgive?
- What if the other person isn't sorry?
- How can I let someone off the hook for doing something *so wrong*?

Biblical counselor June Hunt has been there herself, enabling her to speak from experience as she offers biblical help and hope with heartfelt compassion. If you've been pinned down under a landslide of pain, here's how to find true freedom through forgiveness.

HOW TO HANDLE YOUR EMOTIONS

God created us with the ability to experience emotions. But all too often it's easy for our emotions to get the best of us. Discover how you can bring your emotions under control, and allow God to use them to strengthen you and build up others.

About the Author

June Hunt is founder and CEO of Hope For The Heart (www.HopeForTheHeart.org) and is a dynamic Christian leader who has yielded landmark contributions to the field of Christian counseling. Hope For The Heart provides biblically based counsel in 24 languages in 60 countries on six continents. June, who celebrated 25 years of ministry in 2011, is also an author, speaker, musician, and has served as guest professor to a variety of colleges and seminaries.

Early family pain shaped June's heart of compassion. Her bizarre family background left her feeling hopeless and caused June to contemplate "drastic solutions." But when June entered into a life-changing relationship with Jesus Christ, the trajectory of her life was forever altered. As a result, she grew passionate about helping people face life's tough circumstances.

As a youth director, June became aware of the need for *real* answers to *real* questions. Her personal experiences with pain and her practical experience with youth and parents led June into a lifelong commitment of *Providing God's Truth for Today's Problems*. She earned a master's in counseling at Criswell College in 2007 and has been presented with two honorary doctorates.

Between 1989 and 1992, June Hunt developed and taught *Counseling Through the Bible*, a scripturally based counseling course addressing 100 topics in categories such as marriage and family, emotional entrapments and cults, as well as addictions, abuse, and apologetics. Since then, the coursework has been continually augmented and refined, forming the basis for the *Biblical Counseling Library*. Her *Biblical Counseling Keys* became the foundation of the ministry's expansion, including the 2002 creation of the *Biblical Counseling Institute* (BCI) initiated by Criswell College to equip spiritual leaders, counselors, and other caring people who offer others practical solutions for life's most pressing problems.

The *Biblical Counseling Keys* provide a foundation for the ministry's two daily radio programs, *Hope For The Heart* and *Hope In The Night*, both hosted by June. *Hope For The Heart* is a half-hour of interactive teaching heard on over 100 radio outlets across America, and *Hope In The Night* is June's live two-hour call-in counseling program. Together, both programs air domestically and internationally on more than 1000 stations. In 1986, the National Religious Broadcasters (NRB) honored *Hope For The Heart* as "Best New Radio Program" and awarded it Radio Program of the Year in 1989. Women in Christian Media presented June Hunt with an Excellence in Communications award in 2008. The ministry received NRB's Media Award for International Strategic Partnerships in 2010.

As an accomplished musician, June has been a guest on numerous national TV and radio programs, including NBC's *Today*. She has toured overseas with the USO and has been a guest soloist at Billy Graham crusades. June communicates her message of hope on five music recordings: *Songs of Surrender, Hymns of Hope, The Whisper of My Heart, Shelter Under His Wings*, and *The Hope of Christmas*.

June Hunt's numerous books include *Seeing Yourself Through God's Eyes, How to Forgive... When You Don't Feel Like It, Counseling Through Your Bible Handbook, How to Handle Your Emotions, How to Rise Above Abuse, Bonding with Your Teen through Boundaries, The Answer to Anger, Caring for a Loved One with Cancer* (June is a cancer survivor), *and Hope for Your Heart: Finding Strength in Life's Storms.* She is also a contributor to the *Soul Care Bible* and the *Women's Devotional Bible.*

June Hunt resides in Dallas, Texas, home of the international headquarters of Hope For The Heart.